TAKING HEED TO THE FLOCK

TAKING HEED
TO THE
FLOCK

A Study of the Principles
and Practice of Family Visitation

PETER Y. DE JONG, Ph. D.

Wipf and Stock Publishers
199 West 8th Avenue, Suite 3
Eugene, Oregon 97401

Taking Heed to the Flock
A Study of the Principles and Practice of Family Visitation
By De Jong, Peter Y.
ISBN: 1-59244-449-0
Publication date 12/22/2003
Previously published by Baker Book House, 1948

FOREWORD

Dr. P. Y. De Jong believes that family visitation — for *that* is the subject which he discusses in the following pages — is in danger of declining and dying away in the church of his fathers. He would bewail the loss of this venerable institution and the spiritual values which it represents. His concern has prompted him to take up the cudgel for family visitation. The defense of the practice that is close to his heart, is a labor of love as is evident from the warmth which meets the reader on every page, from the first to the last.

Apart from the question, whether family visitation is losing its hold, it is exceedingly good practice to discuss in a public way those institutions that are typical of our way of life. It is not wise, and it may be dangerous, to take for granted that customs and practices that have long been in vogue will live on indefinitely. It is necessary that we put forth special effort to hold fast that which we have and which we deem worth keeping, if we would retain it, especially if and when contrary winds are blowing. Circumstances often give rise to the question whether we should retain practices that have deep rootage in the past, in times that differ markedly from the age in which such practices had their birth. Of course, this does not apply to ecclesiastical practices that are based squarely and directly on express injunctions of Scripture.

Dr. De Jong has done a good work in looking closely into the merits and warrant of family visitation, in the ten chapters of this volume. The book is interesting reading, and withal informative. It will doubtless command a generous assent to the proposition he lays down, namely, that family visitation should by all means be retained in principle and improved in practice.

May God command His gracious and needful blessing upon this treatise, and thus make it useful in a large measure unto the fruitful performance of family visitation. It will then bring glory to God's name through the increasing spiritual welfare of His flock.

S. VOLBEDA
Professor of Practical Theology
Calvin Seminary,
Grand Rapids, Mich.

February 6, 1948

TABLE OF CONTENTS

PREFACE

Many years ago a travel-worn visitor made his way slowly into the city of Geneva, which lay sparkling like a diamond beside the deep-blue waters of Lac Leman. He had no eye, however, for the physical beauty which greeted him on every hand. Men had told him of the spiritual attractiveness of that town which had made such an enviable reputation for itself throughout Europe.

John Valentin Andrea, preacher and teacher of the holy gospel in Germany, had come to see for himself the beauty of the Genevese republic. He had not been compelled to seek refuge there from the bloody sword of religious persecution. Rather, he was deeply interested in the secret of the spiritual prosperity of Christ's Church in those parts. Like many who had come there before him, he praised the high standard of morals which characterized its citizenry in a luxury-loving and licentious age. And in seeking some explanation for it, he was satisfied to conclude that it resulted chiefly from the regularity and thoroughness which had characterized the family visitation by ministers and elders since the days of Calvin.

To this very day one of the salient features of the Reformed church life is the type of spiritual care and supervision which the officers of the church exercise over the lives of the members. We who may still enjoy the rich fruits of the two great revivals in the Netherlands during the previous century, that of 1834 as well as of 1886, have come to regard annual family visitation as part of our religious heritage. And those who give it more than passing consideration must agree that it has done much to keep the church strong and pure.

This, however, does not exclude the possibility of danger.

Always when a practice has long continued in the churches, signs of degeneration put in their subtle appearance. People gradually lose sight of the meat, and content themselves with the husk.

Unmistakable signs of such an unspiritual attitude on our part toward the venerable institution of family visitation alarm those who know and love our church. Often derogatory remarks are freely made and go unchallenged. Some do not even hesitate to go so far as to denounce it as the fertile breeding-place of hypocrisy in the churches.

As a result this work is not carried on with the same devotion and regularity which characterized its exercise some decades ago. Unless there is a revival of knowledge of, and interest in it, family visitation will soon be relegated to oblivion. Naturally, if the practice has outlived its usefulness for a modern generation, we do well to dispense with it at once. However, it would be folly to pursue such a radical course without considering carefully the place which it was meant to fill in the life of the church. This the author aims to accomplish in these pages. At times he has leaned heavily upon Biesterveld's *Het Huisbezoek,* the study of which has been exceedingly profitable for him.

As far as we have been able to ascertain, no monograph has been written in the American language about this aspect of the official work of the churches. Hence, our elders are particularly at a loss when they must discharge this work which belongs specifically to their office. Lest we lose something which is distinctively Reformed and which has contributed immeasurably to the spiritual strength of our churches, our people should be better informed on the nature, necessity and purpose of family visitation. To meet this need in some small way these pages have been written.

May what has been written here contribute in some measure to a better understanding and deeper appreciation of this worthy practice in our churches. May it assist in the faithful and fruitful execution of this task.

P. Y. DE JONG

THE NAME AND NATURE OF FAMILY VISITATION

"The shepherd has but imperfectly done his work when he has procured for, and administered to his flock, wholesome nourishment. He must watch over them; he must not allow either wolves or goats to mix with them, and, should such find their way among them, he must use appropriate means to get rid of them; he must endeavor to prevent the sheep from straying, and, when they do wander, he must employ every proper method to bring them back; he must endeavor to preserve them from the attacks of disease, and administer suitable preventives and medicines for prevailing maladies; and even at personal hazard he must protect them from those beasts of prey who go about seeking to devour them."

JOHN BROWN: EXPOSITORY DISCOURSES ON FIRST PETER.

One of the most instructive and comforting doctrines of Holy Scripture for the people of God is undoubtedly that of the indivisible spiritual union of Christ and His church. We can no more think of Christ without the church, than we can conceive of the church without Christ.

Especially among Reformed Christians has the conviction of the Lordship of Christ over His spiritual body been influential in molding the government of the organized congregation and the spiritual life of its members. From earliest times, therefore, in our churches it was solemnly confessed that every one who believed was under obligation not only to unite himself with the church but also to place himself and his family under the spiritual care of the under-shepherds who were appointed by the Exalted Savior. For although Christ Himself had ascended to heaven to occupy the place of highest glory and exercise world-wide dominion as a reward upon His obedience to the will of the Father, He in His infinite wisdom and love was pleased for the sake of the good order of His church and the welfare of those for whom He gave His life to institute and maintain to this very day the holy offices.

Onc of these offices, that of the eldership, is particularly concerned with the government of the church. Those to whom this work has been entrusted may find the New Testament replete with counsel and admonition relevant to the faithful discharge of their task. Thus Paul charged the elders at Miletus at the time of his fond farewell, "Take heed unto yourselves, and to all the flock, in which the Holy Spirit hath made you bishops, to feed the church of the Lord which he purchased with his own blood."[1] In much the same vein Peter counsels the elders in the churches to which he wrote, "Tend the flock of God which is among you, exercising the oversight, not of constraint, but willingly, according to the will of God; nor yet for filthy lucre, but of a ready mind; neither as lording it over the charge allotted to you, but making yourselves ensamples to the flock."[2]

It is to the glory of the Reformed churches that they alone throughout the centuries have consistently maintained this office. Whereas in so many churches only ministers of the Word and deacons function as the spiritual leaders of the people, the progeny of the Calvinistic Reformation in imitation of their greatest teacher and leader have insisted on the three offices, each representing in its unique way some aspect of the threefold office of the Savior.

The duty of these elders is to maintain good order and discipline in the church of Christ.

The sphere of their labors embraces the whole visible church of Jesus Christ, old and young alike.

And because the Reformed churches have always had a deep appreciation for the way in which Christ through His Holy Spirit employs the organic relations of human life for the coming of His kingdom, they have from the very beginning of their history conducted family visitation. By this means the churches have been able to wield an influence in the lives of their members as well as in the life of community and nation far in excess of their numerical strength.

As we begin our study of this important aspect of the work of the organized church, we should first carefully consider the name by which it is designated and also understand clearly what is meant by the practice itself.

The Problem of the Name

Those who are at all acquainted with life in the Reformed churches will at one time or another have come across the Holland term

[1] Acts 20:28.
[2] I Peter 5:2, 3.

"huisbezoek." This term, and its English equivalents "home-visitation" or "house-visitation," were lucid enough to win rather general acceptance. They immediately bring to our attention the fact that the church is deeply interested in the lives which her members live from day to day, particularly in the sanctuary of their homes. Not only are living members to make diligent use of the means of grace at the time of public worship, but the church through her officers must maintain a direct and close contact with those whose spiritual care has been entrusted to her by the Lord of the church Himself.

In an attempt to find an appropriate English equivalent for the customary Holland designation our fathers encountered several difficulties. Language is living; has a flavor of its own. It is therefore always hazardous to satisfy oneself with a literal translation of any term. Thus speaking of "home-visitation" or "house-visitation" met with objections.

Many feel, and rightly so, that the church through her officers is not so much interested in the house as a place of habitation as in the family which has taken up residence in some particular place. It is of the very essence of the Reformed religion to stress not the individual as an isolated person but rather the individual in his organic relation to human society. Since the home is the foundation upon which the whole structure of society is built, the proper spiritual contact between the church and her members should be made first of all in the homes. Without ignoring or much less denying the fact that certain problems and difficulties in the lives of individual members will arise which cannot be discussed properly in the presence of others, the Reformed churches have maintained their conviction that under normal circumstances the contact should be sought in and through the family circle. The family consists of those persons who form a household under one head, generally the father. It consists of parents, children, servants (if any), and even such others who may live for a time with these as boarders or friends.

The Term "Visitation"

By some, great objections have been levelled against the second part of the term. They have even preferred using the word "visiting" to the term "visitation," demurring that the latter refers to an unpleasant or calamitous experience resulting from the wrath of God.

A careful consideration of that word, however, ought to dispel such a notion at once. The *New Century Dictionary* lists five distinct uses of the term:

1. the art of visiting; a visit; esp. visiting or a visit for the purpose of making an official inspection or examination.
2. the visit of the Virgin Mary to her cousin Elizabeth; a church festival held on July 2 in commemoration of this visit.
3. a visiting with comfort or aid, or with affliction or punishment, as by God.
4. a special dispensation from heaven, whether of favor or of affliction.
5. any experience or event, especially an unpleasant one, regarded as occurring by divine dispensation; an affliction or punishment from God; a judgment.

From this list it is apparent that no one need object to the term "visitation" at all. The very first meaning given suits our purpose admirably, when casting about for a suitable phrase to describe the work in question. For after all, this work is part of the official program of any well-regulated Reformed church. Every minister and elder installed in the churches assumes part of the responsibility which rests upon the consistory to contact the families entrusted to it, in an official way. Such a call is definitely official, and thus does not depend upon the whims or wishes of either consistory or congregation. And its aim is to make an official inspection or investigation of the lives of the members with a view to ascertaining whether or not they are aware of their spiritual privileges and obligations.

The Name "Consistorial Call"

Some of those who object to the term discussed above have preferred to speak of the "consistorial call." Such a designation has some decided advantages. It tells us at once who is charged with the responsibility of carrying on this important work. The *consistory* is constituted of ruling elders. It should be noted that this body always includes the minister of the Word, since he functions in a double capacity, serving the congregation both as ruling and as teaching elder. He must, therefore, give himself not only to teaching and preaching but also to shepherding and governing the people of God.

In a broad sense the consistory is the court in the Reformed church. Here the rules which must govern the members of the congregation are made and tested, applied and upheld. Thus such a consistorial call is the official visit of the members of the church by an appointed committee of the consistory under whose spiritual jurisdiction they have placed themselves. Thus strictly speaking the elders can carry out this work only with reference to those who are directly under their official supervision, that is, the members of the church by baptism and profession of faith. Others may be counselled by them, since the church must witness to all men, but the officers of the church have no direct spiritual authority over them.

Many arguments can be adduced in favor of this last designation. However, there are also restrictions on the name. Since *calls* are made by committees of the *consistory* for other reasons and with other purposes in mind, it may easily lead to confusion. The term "family visitation" undoubtedly deserves preference, since it emphasizes the official nature of the work, speaks of the Christian family as the object of the work, and as a general designation has been widely used and generally accepted in our churches.

Understanding the Nature of the Work

Although the phrase "family visitation" already describes in a general way the work of the consistory which we are discussing, it is necessary to consider this somewhat more at length.

During the course of the years we have been inclined, particularly in a democratic environment, to minimize the place and necessity of spiritual authority in the church of Christ. As a result too many people cherish erroneous conceptions concerning the right of private judgment in matters of faith and life.

In order that good order may be promoted in the church and that the kingdom of God may be established in the hearts and lives of men, Christ has been pleased to entrust the power of the keys of the kingdom to the officers of the church. By their use those who hear the Word of God may judge whether or not they have a part in the living church.

Our *Belgic Confession,* although using slightly different terminology makes mention of these keys in Article 29, when it speaks of

"The marks of the true church, and wherein it differs from the false church."

> "The marks by which the true church is known are these: If the pure doctrine of the gospel is preached therein; if it maintains the pure administration of the sacraments as instituted by Christ; if church discipline is exercised in the punishing of sin; in short, if all things are managed according to the pure Word of God, all things contrary thereto rejected, and Jesus Christ acknowledged as the only Head of the Church. Hereby the true Church may certainly be known, from which no man has a right to separate himself."

The next three articles elaborate on this subject in such a way that anyone who reads them must conclude that the Reformed churches early placed a high value on the rules of discipline according to which they were to order their lives.

In the *Heidelberg Catechism* an even more elaborate description is given of these keys, which are there considered to be the preaching of the holy gospel and church discipline or excommunication out of the Christian church. To this definition is added the explanation of their use, "By these two the kingdom of heaven is opened to believers and shut against unbelievers." From such definitions it is evident that our Reformed fathers believed that the officers of the church were entrusted with a large measure of spiritual responsibility and clothed with great spiritual authority.

In the Roman Catholic church the idea of the keys of the kingdom had always enjoyed a prominent place. It confessed that the visible church through the hierarchy could open or shut heaven to the individual. In fact, the whole papal system of church government rests upon that assumption.

However, through the centuries the use of the keys of the kingdom in the Roman church had shifted from the preaching of the gospel to the confessional. It was there and there alone that supervision was exercised over the faith and conduct of the believer. Upon such stated occasions the priest, who was clothed with all authority by virtue of his consecration at the hands of a bishop, could interrogate the members, evaluate their spiritual condition and impose the required penalties upon all who erred.

The Reformed churches at the very beginning of their independent existence again restored the preaching of the gospel to its rightful place. However, they claimed that since the church can never know the individual heart except in so far as the individual speaks freely and honestly, the judgment of the church is necessarily conditional. In the last analysis the individual believer must judge whether or not he is right with God and thus meets the conditions which the Word of God demands of all those who claim to be in the faith. But in order that the individual who heard the gospel might be able to examine his heart and life properly in the light of the Word, the Reformed churches early instituted the practice of family visitation.

Making Necessary Distinctions

From this it is evident that family visitation is a unique type of pastoral work carried on by the church of Christ.

It may never degenerate in the direction of becoming a purely social visit for the purpose of paying respects to those who hold membership in the visible church. This seems to be the emphasis in many of the denominations around us. Too often statements are made in which the zeal of a pastor for making such social calls regularly is lauded as the cause of his success in the ministry.

Should family visitation gradually begin to assume this character, we may be sure that the officers have long forgotten their duty laid upon them by the Savior Himself as well as the authority with which He has clothed them for the faithful discharge of the same. History demonstrates that where social demands overshadow the spiritual in the church, spiritual life suffers lamentably and the church of Christ languishes.

We ought to make a careful distinction between family visitation and mutual edification.

The latter ought very definitely assume a large place in our Christian life. It is impossible for the believer who is conscious of the great gift of salvation which he enjoys to refrain from speaking about this to others. The duty of testifying to and confessing Christ before men belongs to the office of all believers. Often the Scriptures speaks of the necessity of "exhorting one another" to faith and good works.

However, family visitation differs radically from this aspect of the life of the living church. It is conducted officially. Although we ought to admonish one another often in the spirit and after the example of Christ, it has not pleased the Head of the church to grant spiritual authority to all. This He has reserved only for the officers. Indeed, as men and brethren of the congregation they are no more important and necessary than any of the other members. Yet by virtue of their holy calling they occupy a unique place and are called to a unique work. They are to tend the flock of God, and in order that they may be able to discharge their duty to the glory of God and the welfare of the church they have received spiritual authority.

In our days of revolution it is not amiss to emphasize often the place and purpose of such spiritual authority in the congregation.

A well-regulated Reformed church can not exist without a knowledge of and acquiescence to the spiritual powers which Christ has conferred upon her elders. When then, they conduct family visitation, they enter the home not merely as fellow-brethren in the faith for the purpose of giving good counsel and bringing consolation. Rather, they are sent out by Christ as the Great Shepherd of His sheep to bring the members of His flock an official message in His behalf.

Such work places a heavy responsibility upon those who are called to perform this task.

All matters with which they must deal are strictly confidential. Theirs is never the duty of prying into the secrets of the heart. Yet they must be able to form some adequate conception of the level of spirituality found among the members of the church. In the true sense of the word their work is that of "shepherding the flock." They must lead and guide, instruct and exhort, warn and comfort all those whom God in His providence has entrusted to their spiritual care.

THE HISTORY OF FAMILY VISITATION

"Any church which forsakes the regular and uniform for the periodical and spasmodic service of God, is doomed to decay; any church which relies for its spiritual strength and growth entirely upon seasons of "revival" will very soon have no genuine revivals to rely on. Our holy God will not conform His blessings to man's moods and moral caprice. If a church is declining, it may need a "revival" to restore it; but what need was there of its declining?"
T. L. CUYLER: RECOLLECTIONS.

"The student is to read history actively and not passively; to esteem his own life the text, and books the commentary. Thus compelled, the muse of history will utter oracles as never to those who do not respect themselves." EMERSON: ESSAYS.

During the first years of the Protestant Reformation the struggle for establishing the true Biblical religion was fierce indeed. Among the bitter calumnies which the reformers had to endure, there was none more contrary to the truth and more grievous to their own hearts, than that they were subverting the good order of Christ's church by insisting upon innovations.

In his beautiful essay on *The Necessity of Reforming the Church*, presented to the Imperial Diet at Spires (A. D. 1544), Calvin's facile pen gives the lie to this accusation. He writes, "Therefore, let there be an examination of our whole doctrine, of our form of administering the sacraments, and our method of governing the Church; and in none of these three things will it be found that we have made any change upon the ancient form, without attempting to restore it to the exact standard of the Word of God."[1]

This attempt has been at once the glory and the strength of the Reformed churches.

More than any other Christian group which arose in those turbulent years, the Reformed sought consciously and consistently to model their church life after the apostolic pattern. Thus in distinction from almost every other party in Christendom they have also maintained and defended the practice of family visitation throughout the years. By pursuing this course of contact with the families of the congregation, the ministers and elders insisted that they were not introducing something new but rather reviving a practice which dated back to the early church. Therefore it is profitable for us,

[1]Calvin's Tracts, Vol. 1, p. 146.

too, to give some attention to the origin and roots of this common practice among us.

Supervision in the Early Church

Already very early in church history we meet with a practice which in some respects may be considered the antecedent of our Reformed family visitation.

Both Clement of Alexandria and Cyprian in their writings offer proof that in their days the officers of the churches visited the members in their homes with some degree of regularity. So too the *Apostolic Constitutions*, when describing the work of the bishop, mention specifically the duty of taking heed to the flock, which included not only seeking those who had gone astray but also encouraging those in the faith who had given no offense because of public sins.

From these and other examples it is evident that the first fathers of the churches did not deem the public instruction given in the church at the time of worship sufficient to meet the demands of spiritual life. They sought to supplement the preaching with a type of spiritual care in which the members were contacted in their homes. Although because of the situation which obtained in those days the emphasis soon fell almost exclusively on the work of discipline, many examples of pastors who took a deep and abiding interest in the needs of their people may be mentioned.

After some centuries the church began to shift the emphasis in the spiritual nurture of the flock. The sacraments were stressed as the chief means of grace, and in connection with this a new view of the significance of the visible church arose which did great damage to the work of visitation. Yet for some centuries the two views continued side by side.

Chrysostom, the most distinguished Christian orator of Constantinople, insisted that in spite of the many difficulties which this task worked, it was essential to the welfare of the churches. Many, he realized, desired such visits by the officers of the church only because they flattered personal pride. Yet in spite of the danger of ministering to and feeding such sinful desires, he felt that all the members should be contacted in their homes. Gregory the Great also understood the value of having the pastors know the conditions and needs of all the members of the flock. In his writings Ambrose of Milan placed a high value on the work, claiming that by giving such guidance to individual souls the priest is fulfilling the work which he began at the administration of the sacraments in public worship. One of the chief regrets of Augustine, the best-known of all these early church fathers, was that he had not given more consideration to pastoral duties, particularly those of shepherding the souls entrusted to his care.

Decline Among the Roman Catholics

Soon after Augustine's day a new theory of the church and the sacraments made rapid headway.

These novel theories concerning the means of grace taught that grace could be wrought in the soul in a mechanical way through a faithful external use of the sacraments. Such a conception naturally left no place for the spiritual care of the members of the church. Thus this work gradually came to be entirely neglected. The glory and power of the mother church rather than the spiritual development of the members was the paramount aim of the priests. The method which was deliberately chosen to attain this goal was the private confessional, by means of which the church was better able to make her members obedient sons and daughters.

The early church, as has been demonstrated conclusively by those who have made careful study of the matter, knew of no private confessional. Indeed, its discipline required a type of public confession of sins and penance, but this differed radically from the practices which became current during the Middle Ages.

Private confession to a priest had its beginnings in the monasteries and cloisters, and only gradually did it force its way into the churches. Nowhere did it receive more wholehearted support than among the Irish monks who as early as the sixth century extended its use to the laity. Here we find also traces of the earliest penitential books, in which proper satisfactions were assessed for certain sins committed.

In many quarters the opposition to this novel practice continued for years. During the reign of Charlemagne there were many places in France which opposed it vehemently. However, the growing influence of the monks presaged the final victory for such private confession. By 1215 the practice had become well-nigh universal, so that the Fourth Lateran Council was able without any significant opposition to legislate on the matter. When once it became canon law, the domination of the priests over the people became an accomplished fact.

As a result of this new practice every Roman Catholic manual on pastoral theology speaks at length of the confessional and its place in the life of the church. It is the heart of the spiritual care which the church exercises over the lives of her members. Everyone is obliged to use the confessional as one of the necessary means of grace. There must, of course, be the reasonable assurance that the individual member is ready and willing to confess all, that he is moved by a genuine repentance and that he purposes to mend his ways. Thereupon, either by listening to the penitent or asking him certain questions, the priest receives the confession. After this is accomplished, he must be competent to judge on the matter of the seriousness of the sins confessed as well as on the restoration which the sinner must make to God, his neighbor and the church. After all this is done, he may by virtue of the juridical authority vested in him pronounce the absolution and impose the penalty. The last consists generally of fasting and prayers and giving alms. At first the aim of this new method of spiritual care was the development of the spiritual life of the believers, but gradually the emphasis fell on the church's prerogative of governing the lives of the members. To execute this matter properly many directives and manuals have been issued during the last centuries which have tended to simplify the work and lighten the responsibility of the individual priest.

Pastoral Care Among the Protestants

For the many hundreds of thousands who during long years had been in spiritual bondage to this system, the Protestant Reformation was the dawn of a new day. Indeed, the reformers did not introduce anything essentially new. Their aim was to purify the church of all the excrescences of the Middle Ages and thus to return to the faith and practice of the apostolic churches. In doctrine, government and worship they broke radically with the deformations which had characterized the life of Christendom for centuries and brought a real measure of spiritual liberty to the people of God. This work was begun by Luther and his disciples and reached its richest development under Calvin and those who followed him.

In many respects the Lutheran Reformation was still partial and inconsistent. As spiritual leader Luther himself sought to retain as many of the forms and traditions as possible by merely removing the vicious elements and improving what remained. The question which he and others raised was not whether the practice under discussion enjoyed solid Scriptural foundation but rather whether it could contribute to the spiritual edification of the church. This approach was also taken when considering the question of the pastoral care of God's people. As a result private confession was retained, although it differed widely from the form current in the Roman church. Early Lutheran confessional writings make mention of it repeatedly and insist that the individual must know whether or not he enjoys the absolution.

During the period of the Thirty Years' War (1618-1648), when most of Germany was hopelessly divided and tragically devastated, the Lutheran churches experienced a period of spiritual poverty and decline. At that time private confession fell into disuse and never again occupied a place of importance in the churches. However, the public service of confession was still continued as part of the proper preparation for the celebration of the Lord's Supper. Although many early as well as later Lutheran pastors set a worthy example in their faithfulness in visiting the sick and needy, the church never introduced official family visitation. The chief cause for this neglect must be undoubtedly sought in the Lutheran neglect of the office of ruling elder in the congregations.

Family Visitation Among the Reformed

At the outset the Reformed churches under the able leadership of John Calvin broke completely with the system of confessional and the sacrament of penance. They returned to the time-honored practice of visiting the members in their homes. This they also developed to a much higher degree than ever before in the history of the Christian church, no doubt as a result of carefully maintaining the office of the ruling elders in every congregation.

Already at an early date Calvin emphasized that pastoral work included far more than official preaching of the gospel. He insisted on faithfulness on the part of all the pastors in visiting the members of the church, since he realized how beneficial this work was for the development of spiritual life and the edification of the church. Those

Reformed leaders who came to Geneva during that time and saw the progress which had been made began to follow the same pattern of church care. Thus the practice of family visitation became current wherever Reformed churches were established.

In Geneva the work was carried on with great regularity. Four times a year, before each celebration of the Lord's Supper, all the members were to be visited in their homes by the ministers and the elders. Special attention was given to the young people, in order that they might prepare themselves for profession of their faith and thus receive the right to use the Lord's Supper. Some have argued that all this was merely part of the iron-clad discipline which Calvin imposed on the town. However, this assertion rests upon a double misunderstanding. First of all, family visitation was regarded as definitely part of the church's calling towards her members. It had little if anything to do with the civil government of the city. Then too, the reformers made a careful and judicious distinction between family visitation and church discipline. The purpose of the former was never to pry into the hearts of the individuals but rather to exhort and stimulate the believers to a life of sanctification in all its parts. Especially the churches in the Netherlands and Scotland have sought to follow this same practice diligently, in some groups to our very day.

It is therefore a mistaken notion to argue that our Reformed fathers, having rid the churches of the confessional, felt the need of some substitute and hence introduced family visitation. In no sense of the word is the latter a substitute for the former. Rather, in their heroic attempt to purify the church of Christ of unscriptural practices they returned to the Bible and found there a solid foundation for this type of spiritual work. Too long had the church through its leaders ignored an important aspect of her calling. And only by restoring and maintaining the proper spiritual contact between the church's officers and her members were they able to rejoice in an evident revival of spiritual life in the congregations.

THE SCRIPTURAL BASIS OF FAMILY VISITATION

"The church is not only not bound to be guided by any other rule or standard, but is not at liberty to have regard to any other; as this would be virtually to withdraw herself from subjection to Christ's authority, and voluntarily to submit to a foreign yoke. No mere laws or statutes of men — no mere regard to worldly or secular advantages — should ever regulate the conduct of the church of Christ, or of any section or branch of it. She should be guided solely by the revealed will of Christ, and she should ascertain what that will is by diligent and prayerful study of His word."

WILLIAM CUNNINGHAM: HISTORICAL THEOLOGY.

Although it is both appropriate and valuable to know something about the history of the venerable custom of conducting family visitation, we who are Reformed realize full well that it is of far greater consequence to consider whether or not the practice has the approval of the Holy Scriptures.

For surely if this spiritual activity is rooted merely in the whims and fancies of men, it can accomplish little if any lasting good. Then those who engage in it are arrogating to themselves spiritual functions and powers which do not belong to them by right. Should purely practical concerns move the church to carry on this work, we are convinced that the practice could not long continue and much less carry away the indispensable blessing of God. Sound practice can result only from sound theory. Therefore if there is no Scriptural foundation for this work, the sooner we rid ourselves of it as an improper as well as an unnecessary encumbrance, the more readily the spiritual life of the congregation will develop in a wholesome direction.

The Biblical View of the Church

In order to answer the question under consideration it will be necessary first of all to have regard for what God's Word teaches us concerning the church.

The Bible never wearies of informing us that the church is the spiritual body of the Savior. Paul in the epistle to the Ephesians speaks of "the church, which is his body, the fulness of him that filleth all in all."[1] Her life is entirely bound up with Christ Himself,

[1]Ephesians 1:22,23.

for He is 'the Head, from whom all the body, being supplied and knit together through the joints and bands, increaseth with the increase of God."[1]

Reformed Christians have therefore always insisted that all the activities of the church must find their justification in the blue-prints which God has provided for well-regulated congregational life. These are found only in His inspired Word. The church is not the product of the mind or will of man. Instead of believing that the organization owes her being to religiously-minded men and women who have voluntarily united themselves in a visible society, we confess that the church has been established and is maintained by Christ through His Holy Spirit.

Thus we agree with the statement of the *Belgic Confession,* which reads, "We believe and profess one catholic or universal Church, which is a holy congregation of true Christian believers, all expecting their salvation in Jesus Christ, being washed by His blood, sanctified and sealed by the Holy Spirit."[2] Likewise the *Heidelberg Catechism* in answering the question "What do you believe concerning the holy catholic church?" replies, "That the Son of God, out of the whole human race, from the beginning to the end of the world, gathers, defends, and preserves for Himself, by His Spirit and Word, in the unity of the true faith, a Church chosen to everlasting life; and that I am, and forever shall remain, a living member thereof."[3]

In order that those who are such members may attain to spiritual manhood and womanhood, Christ has been pleased to institute the offices in His church. Through them as the usual means which He is pleased to employ, He works for their salvation.

Thus all the activities performed by them must be done in His name and according to His will. The work of ministers, elders and deacons is in a very real sense the work of Christ accomplished by them. They have been officially called and qualified for their task. And, as they engage in it, the members of the congregation must recognize in their labors of love and patience the ceaseless work of Christ on their behalf.

Is family visitation, then, based on a solid Scriptural foundation? In the light of the teaching of Holy Writ on the relation of Christ to

[1]Colossians 2:19.
[2]Article 27.
[3]Lord's Day XXI, 54.

His church, of the church to its officers, and of these officers to the Savior Himself we firmly believe that it is.

Christ as Our Chief Shepherd

The Bible teaches us that the great work which Christ does on behalf of His church is basically pastoral. He is first and foremost the Great Shepherd of His sheep.

This very name, so rich in meaning and inexhaustible in comfort, is applied to Him in the benediction found at the close of the epistle written to the Hebrews. "Now the God of peace, that brought again from the dead our Lord Jesus, that great Shepherd of the sheep, through the blood of the everlasting covenant . . ."[1] The Savior refers to Himself similarly, "I am the good shepherd: the good shepherd layeth down his life for the sheep."[2]

Such passages teach us that He has been sent by the Father into this world, in order that He might seek and save His own. As a faithful shepherd He brings them together into one flock and leads them by His Spirit and Word. With loving care and tenderness He watches over them all, lest any go astray. And when one has wandered from the safety of the fold, He leaves the ninety and nine to seek him who because of waywardness has forfeited the safety of the flock and is in danger of his life on the wild mountainsides of the world. Even as a shepherd by virtue of his calling is obligated to provide food and drink for the sheep, lead them into pleasant pastures and defend them against all enemies, so Christ as the Good Shepherd guarantees that all the needs of His own will be abundantly supplied. He has purchased His flock not with gold or silver or precious stones but with His life-blood. Therefore in life and death they are not their own but belong with both body and soul to Him.

That unique ownership of Christ is stressed in several of Paul's epistles. We read, "For ye are bought with a price: therefore glorify God in your body, and in your spirit, which are God's."[3] In the next chapter a similar exhortation is expressed, "Ye are bought with a price; be ye not the servants of men."[4] Thus in the sight of God He rules His people with perfect right. He alone is their Head and

[1]Hebrews 13:20.
[2]John 10:11.
[3]I Corinthians 6:20.
[4]I Corinthians 7:23.

King, and the holy obligation of all who belong to His flock is to render constant and loving obedience to His will.

From this we must conclude that the church is in no position to rule and care for herself. It is both her glory and the guarantee of her safety that she belongs to another. In our days when we hear so often of the right of the church to make her own rules, how necessary it is to remember that the life of God's people must be grounded entirely in the unique relationship which obtains between them and their Shepherd.

The Undershepherds Whom He Appoints

When we consider the Scriptural basis for family visitation, we must always bear in mind also the relation in which the members of the church stand to the officers.

Since Christ has ascended into heaven, He has been carrying out His triple office from the place of highest glory and power at the right hand of the Father. This He does in a double way — not only through the immediate operation of the Holy Spirit in the hearts of those chosen to eternal life, but also mediately through human agents appointed by Himself in connection with the express choice of the members of the congregation themselves. These are the officers of the church. In distinction from the deacons, who also have certain pastoral duties to perform, it has pleased the Head of the church to charge the elders as undershepherds of the flock to watch for the souls.

Paul speaks in this vein of the diversity of gifts which Christ has communicated to His people. "And He gave some to be apostles; and some, prophets; and some, evangelists; and some, pastors and teachers; for the perfecting of the saints, unto the work of ministering, unto the building up of the body of Christ."[1] Likewise in the epistle to the Corinthians he counsels the believers to submit themselves to all who labor in the work of ministering to the saints. The attitude of those who enjoy this spiritual care may be inferred from the plain teaching of Hebrews 13:17, "Obey them that have the rule over you, and submit to them: for they watch in behalf of your souls, as they that shall give account; that they may do this with joy, and not with grief: for this were unprofitable for you."

[1]Ephesians 4:11, 12.

The same apostle charged Titus with setting in order those things in the church at Crete which were still lacking, thus appointing elders in every city that the churches might prosper. The story of the election of the first deacons speaks of the express choice of the believers in the matter, although the work was carried on under the direct supervision of the apostles as the rulers of the church.

No one can read the New Testament with any degree of care and without prejudice and still deny the necessity of officers in the church. In order that the work of edification may prosper, it is essential that the spiritual power of Christ be vested in certain men chosen to be leaders and examples of the flock. They must perform their duties in the spirit and according to the example of the Savior, being clothed with humility and always ready to serve, and it is incumbent upon the members of the congregation to submit themselves willingly and cheerfully to such government as unto the Lord.

The Responsibility of the Officers to Christ

Yet one more consideration calls for our attention. To establish the Scripturalness of family visitation, it will be necessary to see clearly the relation in which the officers as undershepherds stand to Christ.

Contrary to the popular construction that elders and deacons are the servants of the church and its members, the Bible teaches that they are responsible not first of all to men but rather to the Exalted Savior Himself. This is the plain implication of Hebrews 13:17, where mention is made of the account which each must render of his work. Paul likewise teaches this, when he speaks of himself as being zealous with a godly zeal for the spiritual advancement of the church.

Indeed, because the members are anointed with the Holy Ghost to be prophets, priests and kings and must therefore perform the duties inherent in the office of all believers, the officers of the church are their servants. But as Paul plainly teaches, they are "your servants for Jesus' sake."

Knowing that their calling has come from Christ, the officers may often be compelled to act contrary to the wishes of many in the congregation, in order that they may be able to give a good account of their stewardship in this respect. They must watch carefully, as

Peter warns, lest they arrogate to themselves powers which are not rightfully theirs or make misuse of the position to which they have been lawfully called of God. Never may they lord it over the flock in an attempt to force their will on the believers. But as they perform their work in the spirit of love and with patience, they must be aware that they are ambassadors of God and servants of Christ.

It is true that in this survey we have nowhere discovered a text which speaks directly of family visitation. However, beyond the shadow of a doubt we have seen that the officers must do far more than preach and teach the Word in public worship. They are under-shepherds appointed by Christ, and these must watch for the souls of God's people in the name of Christ Himself. This work demands careful supervision of the faith and conduct of those who name the name of our Lord. This they do in the name of Christ, because of the abiding interest which the Savior sustains in the welfare of His flock. Thus in approaching the believers the elders come not merely with good advice and counsel, but being clothed with authority they must instruct and admonish, warn and comfort. Their words, when conforming to the Word of God, come with the official authority of Him whom they represent; and all who refuse to submit to such good government in the church do violence to the welfare of their souls and cannot, while in such a state, experience the blessing of the Lord.

THE SPIRITUAL PURPOSE OF FAMILY VISITATION

"The first foundation of discipline is to provide for private admonition; that is, if any one does not do his duty spontaneously, or behaves insolently, or lives not quite honestly, or commits something worthy of blame, he must allow himself to be admonished; and every one must study to admonish his brother when the case requires. Here especially is there occasion for the vigilance of pastors and presbyters, whose duty is not only to preach to the people, but to exhort and admonish from house to house, whenever their hearers have not profited sufficiently by general teaching; as Paul shows, when he relates that he taught 'publicly, and from house to house,' and testifies that he is 'pure from the blood of all men,' because he had not shunned to declare 'all the counsel of God' (Acts xx: 20, 26, 27). Then does doctrine obtain force and authority, not only when the minister publicly expounds to all what they owe to Christ, but has the right and means of exacting this from those whom he may observe to be sluggish or disobedient to his doctrine."

JOHN CALVIN: INSTITUTES OF THE CHRISTIAN RELIGION.

To consider the purpose of any activity is always a very important matter, since it is purpose which gives meaning to life. Ruskin has aptly said, "There is no action so slight, nor so mean, but it may be done to a great purpose, and ennobled therefore; nor is any purpose so great but that slight actions may help it, and may be so done as to help it much, most especially that chief of all purposes, the pleasing of God."

Before we therefore dismiss family visitation with a wave of the hand as ineffective and wasteful of time and energy, let us pause to consider its purpose. This alone may be able to convince us of its value in the life of a Reformed church, especially when we bear in mind the development of true spirituality as a means to glorifying our God.

It is apparent at once that our conception of this spiritual ministry of the church is largely governed by our views of the nature and growth of spiritual life. Here again the uniqueness of the Reformed position is clearly demonstrated when compared with the views held by other Christian groups.

Types of Christian Piety

The Roman Catholics who never weary of emphasizing that they alone represent the true continuation of the apostolic church, have adopted as their chief purpose in working among the members of their communion, the welfare of the instituted church. According to them the institution is always of far greater significance than the individual. Gregory the First, one of the most influential popes ever to occupy the see of Peter, clearly presents this as his conception, when he argues that the purpose of all spiritual work among the members is that they may be able to order their lives according to the will of the church. This idea was strongly stressed during the Middle Ages, when the life of the individual was completely wrapped up in that of the church. The pope received the distinct honor of being regarded as the vicar or undershepherd of Christ, and all those who were saved owed him obedience. Any who dared to flaunt the authority of the church were severely dealt with, as many instances of ecclesiastical discipline prove.

During the modern era the Jesuits have done much to perpetuate the influence of the church by their insistence upon obedience. By making auricular confession obligatory upon all the members at least once each year and teaching that salvation can only be found within the walls of the visible church, the Roman Catholic church has firmly bound her members to the organization and to this very day exerts a tremendous influence over their lives.

In the days of the Reformation the emphasis once more was made to fall on personal faith. Luther particularly stressed justification by faith only, which was to be preached as the heart of the gospel. However, in order that the people might clearly see the necessity of a diligent use of the means of grace, he retained the confessional. By means of its regular use for a time the influence of the church in the lives of her members remained dominant. Although he paved the way for the development of pastoral work by insisting on regular visitation of the sick and the needy, he did not grasp the significance of regular spiritual work among the families. Thus the Lutheran membership, far more than the Reformed, has been inclined to satisfy itself with a rather passive faith which accepts the teaching of the church and thus has failed to see the implications of the gospel for daily Christian living.

The present-day Fundamentalists, whose theory and practice betrays close kinship with that of the Anabaptists of the sixteenth century and that of the Pietists of the eighteenth century, have emphasized the individual at the expense of the church and the family. With their "passion for souls" they have encompassed land and sea to bring others to Jesus, forgetting often that the lives of those who have been brought must also grow and develop to spiritual maturity.

Because the Fundamentalists believe that all teaching must root in the heart, they have little appreciation for the official preaching of the gospel. As a result the New Testament regard for the place of officers in the congregation has not come to its own among them. Believing that the congregation is a voluntary association of experiential Christians, they insist that all are clothed with equal authority. Thus there is much room for mutual edification but none for the official visitation of the members by the authorities of the church.

Likewise, their insistence on personal piety has often been so onesided, that the implications of the Christian message of salvation for the whole of life have altogether too easily been overlooked and ignored. (This is the main contention of a recent work by Dr. Carl F. H. Henry entitled *The Uneasy Conscience of Modern Fundamentalism,* which has occasioned much debate in those circles.) The result has been very little appreciation for Christian education in the schools and for Christian action in the spheres of politics, industry and culture.

Much of this can best be explained by the fact that the Fundamentalists, quite like their forerunners some centuries ago, have little appreciation for the Biblical conception of the relation between nature and grace. In their estimation the believer is a "new creature" in Christ in the most radical sense of the term. He must necessarily live a dualistic life as long as he in this world, accommodating himself to life as he finds it for the time being. Since it lies under the curse of God and the power of sin, nothing in it can be restored to the service of Christ and the glory of God. The sole hope of those who believe is regarded to be the imminent return of the Saviour, who at His coming will make all things new and give the believer a redeemed sphere in which his life can become completely integrated.

The Reformed churches have consciously sought to avoid the pitfalls inherent in the conceptions outlined above. As a result of their peculiar insight into the fulness of the gospel of Jesus Christ and its cosmic implications, they have tried to apply their principles to every relationship in which they were involved. To live by the rule of the gospel so completely is an arduous task. It requires not merely preaching the full counsel of God but likewise an appreciation on the part of the believers of the many-sidedness of the gospel message. Christians who were called upon to carry out the will of God at all times felt themselves particularly in need of instruction and encouragement, and to meet this need family visitation was instituted and maintained.

Developing Spiritual Life

The first conscious aim of Reformed family visitation is the development of the spiritual life of the individual.

The importance of this has been seen clearly by the Rev. J. J. Knap, outstanding pastor of one of the large Reformed churches in the Netherlands, who in his little volume on *Spiritual Growth* writes, "The church is duty bound to be a blessing to the world. But how can she be, if her members have no growing, energetic spiritual life? The influence of the church in the world rises or falls with the inner power of its members. The energizing Spirit, from whom a renewing power goes out upon the world through the preaching of the Word, does not live in temples made with hands, but in living hearts which are woven together with the strands of faith and love."[1]

The uniqueness of the life which the Father has given us through the Son by the operation of the Holy Spirit requires much spiritual care, if it is to flourish and bear fruit. Salvation is never our work, but God's alone. Since we are by nature dead in sin, it is impossible for us to turn to God apart from the regenerating operation of the Holy Spirit. His work has so beautifully and accurately been described for us in the *Canons of Dort*:

> "But when God accomplishes His good pleasures in the elect, or works in them true conversion, He not only causes the gospel to be externally preached to them, and powerfully illumines their minds by His Holy Spirit, that they may rightly understand and discern the things of the Spirit of God; but by the efficacy of the

[1]Knap: *Spiritual Growth*, p. 19.

same regenerating Spirit He pervades the inmost recesses of man; He opens the closed and softens the hardened heart, and circumcises that which was uncircumcised; infuses new qualities into the will, which, though heretofore dead, He quickens; from being evil, disobedient and refractory, He renders it good, obedient and pliable; actuates and strengthens it, that like a good tree, it may bring forth the fruits of good actions."[2]

Faith, thus, is far more than knowledge of and assent to the teachings of the church. It is rather the exercise of that personal religious fellowship which the believer has with God through Jesus Christ. The activity of faith is the result of God's renewal of the entire life of the individual. And this must grow and increase, even as Peter admonishes his readers to "grow in the grace and in the knowledge of the Lord Jesus Christ."[3]

All who live by the power of faith consecrate their lives entirely in His service. Yet since the power of sin is never wholly removed in this life, the believer finds within himself a daily conflict. Time and again he is tempted to indulge in the lusts of the flesh, and often he stumbles and falls. Such sins, though fully pardoned by God on the grounds of the efficacy of the atoning work of Christ, nevertheless leave their scars and render the Christian's witness less effectual than it might be. Often the believers will doubt the sincerity of their faith and consequently of their saving relationship to God through Christ. Periods of spiritual darkness and barrenness may darken the light of their souls. In fact, a child of God may stray so far from the blessed communion, that for a time he seems completely callous to the demands of the divine law and the joy of salvation.

In such circumstances, which are by no means rare among God's people, the church must minister to the individual. In order that the tender plant of faith may again be revived and bring forth fruit in its season, the Word must be personally administered and applied. Though the Holy Spirit can alone render these labors effectual, we are to remember that He makes use of human agents. By wise and patient exhortation and rebuke the elders of the church help the believers to "lift up the hands that hang down, and the palsied knees

[2]Chapter III-IV, 11.
[3]II Peter 3:18.

. . . . that that which is lame be not turned out of the way, but rather be healed."[1]

Challenging the Lives of Believers to Service

God's people have a peculiar calling in this world. They are the salt of the earth and the light of the world. In their every endeavor they must show forth the excellencies of Him who called them out of darkness to His marvelous light.

However, to meet this challenge their spiritual life must be not only strong but also active. Faith demands expression; it must be translated into effective Christian service.

Contrary to the emphasis of many Christian groups, the Reformed churches have always insisted that spiritual life, as well as natural, is organic in character. By this is meant that the believer does not and cannot live in isolation. Salvation is far more than a matter of securing and enjoying personal peace with God. It indeed governs our individual relation to God, but just as surely and completely must it give direction to our relation to our fellow-men in all areas of society. The principles of the second table of the law are also regulative for the life of the New Testament believer. We must not only love God above all but also our neighbors as ourselves.

Thus Christian calling embraces all of life. No part of our daily walk lies outside the scope of our faith-relation to God. This follows from the plain Scriptural teaching that God loved "the world", that is, the *created order,* and redeemed it to Himself through the Son of His eternal love. Never for a moment should we forget the intimate relation between nature and grace. The latter aims to restore the former, to reconcile the whole created order to the God who has fashioned it for His own glory. And, although the full realization of that divine program of cosmic salvation will not be seen and enjoyed fully until God Himself makes the new heavens and the new earth in which dwells righteousness, already in this life the first principles of it must become evident in the attitudes and actions of His people.

Such is the comprehensive calling of every believer.

Of this he must be constantly reminded, and to this he must be repeatedly challenged.

And although the preaching of the gospel will provide the chief opportunity of pursuing this course, the Reformed churches have

[1]Hebrews 12:12, 13.

used family visitation as an additional means to challenge the lives of their members. When that challenge personally confronts the believers in their daily walk, we may confidently expect them to utter the prayer

"Fill Thou my life, O Lord, my God,
  In every part with praise,
That my whole being may proclaim
  Thy being and Thy ways.
Not for the lip of praise alone,
  Nor e'en the praising heart,
I ask, but for a life made up
  Of praise in every part."

Promoting the Communion of the Saints

Such a well-rounded Christian life needs much encouragement and help in its daily struggle. To enjoy this the believer must live in the closest possible relationship to the officers and members of the church.

God has been pleased to use means for working out His plan of redemption. Therefore He has established His church among men. In that organization there are many members, each having received unique talents and enjoying a unique position. Paul therefore likens the church to a body, a spiritual unity or organism. Each member is necessary to the well-being of all the others, and is in duty bound to employ his gifts and talents for the advantage of the whole. Knap has described this beautifully, "If we had been created as so many separate entities, without any living connection with the millions of men, we would not need each other for the development of our gifts and powers. All human beings would have many traits of similarity. But the inner relationship would be lacking. Every one would be living as it were, on some glass non-conductor. And that would cut off the possibility of giving spiritual and moral strength to one another."[1] Now, however, God has made us of one blood. In Christ the relationship which was broken by sin has been restored. And in consequence we must remember the law of spiritual growth. "Not in isolation, but in the full flowing stream of life, full-grown personalities are formed."[2]

[1]Knap: *Spiritual Growth*, p. 115, 116.
[2]Ibid, p. 117.

In an age in which individualism is rampant and has wreaked havoc everywhere, it is essential to stress the organic aspect of life. We cannot live without each other. Nowhere is this more valid than in the church among the communion of saints.

Where this law of life is understood, the elders do not regard themselves as policemen of the congregation. Theirs is not the duty of trying to uncover all the sins which mar the hearts of God's people who as yet are imperfect. But, realizing the almost insurmountable obstacles in the way of a well-rounded Christian life, they visit the families for the purpose of helping all to see their duty more clearly. This makes for the closest possible fellowship between the officers and members of the church on the one hand and between the members among each other on the other. They learn to stand shoulder to shoulder in the great spiritual struggle against the common foe and learn to wage this war more successfully. It makes of the church truly a "militant" church. As each soldier has his own position and duty and obliges himself to carry it out in strict obedience to the commands of his superior, so too in the church all the members find their calling outlined by Christ in His Word. The purpose of the work of the elders is to remind the believers in the name of the Commander-in-Chief of their personal and social responsibilities. Where this is found, the words of the well-known hymn are immortalized in the life of the congregation

"Like a mighty army
  Moves the church of God;
Brothers, we are treading
  Where the saints have trod.
We are not divided,
  All one body we,
One in hope and doctrine,
  One in charity."

As this is progressively realized in the life of the church, she marches forward from victory to victory in the name of the Captain of her salvation.

THE NECESSITY OF FAMILY VISITATION

"To be a dutiful undershepherd is, in another view, to be a faithful sheep, following the Chief Shepherd withersoever He goes. Pastors are not lords over God's heritage, but mere servants of Christ, the great Head of the Church, bound to regard His will as their law, and His life as their model . . .

"It is well that our Lord made this plain by the words addressed to the representative man among the apostles; for Christians of active, energetic, and earnest natures are very apt to have very exaggerated ideas of their responsibilities, and to take on themselves the care of the whole world, and impose on themselves the duty of remedying every evil that is done under the sun."

A. B. BRUCE: THE TRAINING OF THE TWELVE.

Perhaps many of us can hardly imagine that a Reformed Christian would ever doubt the value of a practice like family visitation which enjoys such a venerable history and is inspired by such a worthy spiritual aim.

And yet we have such individuals among us, no doubt many more than we are willing to acknowledge.

They contend, and their contention is not devoid of some merit, that the aims of this spiritual work can better be attained in other ways. It is therefore not without reason that we briefly look into the matter of the necessity of family visitation.

Preaching and the Christian Life

In arguing that this practice has long ago outlived its usefulness, these individuals put forth the claim that the triple purpose of encouraging faith, pointing out the believer's Christian obligations and promoting the proper relation between the individual and the church can be attained and should be attained through the preaching of the gospel.

None of us will dispute that the preaching and teaching of God's Word is paramount in the development of spiritual life. It is the chief means of grace, to which is appended the administration of the sacraments. The New Testament emphasizes the relation of the believer's life to the means of grace upon many occasions. Already of the church at the time of Pentecost we read that "they continued steadfastly in the apostles' doctrine and fellowship, and in breaking of bread, and in prayers."[1] By doing this, so we read further on in the same chapter, they received the benefits of eating their meat in gladness and singleness of heart and of enjoying favor with all the people. Likewise the writer to the Hebrews warns his readers against forsaking the public gatherings of God's people which contributed greatly to the building up of their faith.

That the strengthening of spiritual life is most intimately bound up with a faithful use of the means of grace has always been believed and strongly urged by our Reformed fathers. In the *Canons of Dort* they propounded their view of the matter in this language:

> "As the almighty operation of God whereby He brings forth and supports this our natural life does not exclude but rather require the use of means by which God, of His infinite mercy and goodness, has chosen to exert His influence, so also the aforementioned supernatural operation of God by which we are regenerated in no wise excludes or subverts the use of the gospel, which the most wise God has ordained to be the seed of regeneration and food of the soul. Wherefore as the apostles and teachers who succeeded them piously instructed the people concerning this grace of God, to His glory and to the abasement of all pride, and in the meantime, however, neglected not to keep them, by the holy admonitions of the gospel, under the influence of the Word, the sacraments, and ecclesiastical discipline; so even now should it be far from those who give or receive instruction in the Church to presume to tempt God by separating what He of His good pleasure has most intimately joined together. For grace is conferred by means of admonitions; and the more readily we perform our duty, the more clearly this favor of God, working in us, usually manifests itself, and the more directly His work is advanced; to whom alone all the glory, both for the means and for their saving fruit and efficacy, is forever due. Amen."[2]

Those therefore who reject the means of grace, specifically the proclamation of the gospel and the administration of the sacraments, do despite to their own souls and despise the gracious gifts of God.

Supervision as the Outreach of Preaching

Such an emphasis on the official preaching of the Word and all that which is connected therewith, however, should in no way be

[1]Acts 2:42.
[2]Chapter III-IV, 17.

understood to exclude official work of a more restricted and personal nature.

We have already pointed out that from the very beginning of the history of the Christian churches many leaders insisted that for the sake of the well-being of spiritual life something additional was necessary. That the work of the elders even in the apostolic age was not restricted to the public gatherings is plainly taught by James in the epistle which he wrote to the churches. "Is any among you sick? let him call for the elders of the church; and let them pray over him, anointing him with oil in the name of the Lord: and the prayer of faith shall save him that is sick, and the Lord shall raise him up; and if he have committed sins, it shall be forgiven him."[1]

That the members of the congregation might receive this personal supervision by the elders, the early leaders of the Reformed churches enjoined a system of family visitation at their first synodical (broader) gathering. Monsma and Van Dellen in their valuable *The Church Order Commentary* offer the following translation of the article which governed that work:

> "They (the Elders) shall faithfully investigate whether they (the Church members) manifest themselves uprightly in walk and conduct, in the duties of godliness, in the faithful instruction of their households in the matter of family prayers, (morning and evening prayers) and such like matters; they shall admonish them to these duties with consideration, but also in all seriousness and according to conditions and circumstances; they shall admonish them to steadfastness, or strengthen them to patience, or spur them on to a serious minded fear of God; such as need comfort and admonition they shall comfort and admonish, and if need be they shall report a matter to their fellow Elders, who together with them are appointed to exercise discipline; and besides these matters they shall correct that which can be corrected according to the gravity of the sin committed; nor shall they neglect, each one in his own district, to encourage them to send their children to catechism."[2]

Although the Synod of The Hague (1586) deemed this article too long for incorporation into the Church Order and greatly abridged it, the chief contents were retained together with specific mention

[1]James 5:14, 15.
[2]Monsma and Van Dellen: *Church Order Commentary*, p. 110.

of official family visitation. In harmony with this our present Order in Article 23 insists that one of the duties of the elders is "for the edification of the Churches to visit the families of the Congregation, in order particularly to comfort and instruct the members, and also to exhort others in respect to the Christian Religion." The last could be done both at the time of family visitation, if such occasions arose, or whenever any opportunity presented itself to them.

It is almost superfluous to add that all this work was regarded as an extension of the proclamation of the gospel. The officers of the church were called to bring to the attention of all those under their jurisdiction the holy demands of their Covenant God and to enjoin them to take seriously the demands of the gospel of salvation.

Arguments for the Necessity of Family Visitation

Is this work, then, necessary for the spiritual well-being of the church of Christ? We are deeply convinced that it is and, chiefly, for the following reasons.

First of all, by means of this custom the elders in the churches are able to carry out the mandate of God's Word which insists upon the duty of watching for the souls of the believers and their children.

This part of their calling should weigh heavily upon all who are called to the sacred office. Christ has bought His church with His precious blood and guaranteed to her all the benefits of His atoning work. However, He has been pleased to leave her here for a while in a wicked and perverse world, in order that she might give a living witness to the power of divine grace. In this world there are countless enemies, appearing in many guises and forms, all of whom would, if possible, seek to lead her astray on the road of ruin. Although Christ is clothed with all authority and thus guards and defends His Church with His almighty power, He is pleased to make use of human agents as His representatives. They are to point out the enemies and present the antidote of the gospel. They must with perseverance and patience exhort all to a life of faith and obedience. They should, above all, constantly remind the people, who are bought with the price, of their heavenly inheritance and the rich grace of the Savior which alone is able to keep them standing in the evil day.

If this work is to be carried out effectively, the elders must know the spiritual conditions and needs of the flock over which they have been placed. How can this ever be done, unless there is some form of intimate contact between the officers and members of the congregation? One day each elder must give account of the stewardship entrusted to him, and in that certain knowledge none can fail to be deeply impressed with the seriousness and solemnity of his charge. Until it is proved that there exists some better form of supervision than that of family visitation, we do well not only to safeguard this institution for future generations by faithfully discharging it but also to improve it constantly by studying and discussing its nature and methods.

Moreover, if we understand the high spiritual purpose of Reformed preaching, we will appreciate the necessity of this practice at once.

We believe that the principles of the gospel never change. They are valid everywhere and under all circumstances. However, because spiritual conditions and needs vary greatly with individuals and times, the particular emphasis of the preaching will change occasionally.

All true gospel preaching consists of exposition and application, that is, of the explanation of the meaning of God's Word and indicating the use to which it must be put in our lives. These are not two separate items in the sermon but closely related and interwoven as the objective and subjective aspects of the same gracious word of life. In order that the second element may rightly come to its own, it is essential that the elders who supervise the preaching of the minister also understand the condition of the congregation. Effective preaching must be specific and pointed. Glittering generalities cannot edify the people of God. The gospel must make a deep and permanent impression upon the lives of those who hear. Only then may we hope for the much-needed fruit.

But how shall the elders know whether or not the preaching is edifying and fruitful, unless they visit the members from time to time in their homes? Throughout the history of the churches it has been demonstrated that there is no better means to a rather adequate knowledge of the spiritual condition of God's people than that presented by family visitation.

Let those who are called to carry on this work be guided by the spirit of love and helpfulness, indeed, having an eye for the reflection of God's glory through the lives of the believers. Let the members of the church be ready and even eager to discuss the power of the gospel in the lives of themselves and the members of their families.

Then the spiritual level of the congregation may be discerned with a fair measure of accuracy, and the minister of the Word will be able to preach the gospel in such a way that with God's blessing it will meet the needs of saints and sinners alike.

But if any now reply that this work of supervision can be better discharged by calling upon the members individually, we would answer that such a method cannot do justice to a very important aspect of spiritual life.

All life is *organic,* that is, it exists in relationship to other, similar lives. Thus spiritual life, too, cannot be treated in isolation. It is not to be considered a hot-house plant, some exotic bloom that flourishes only in the secret recesses of the heart. It must come to expression in daily contact with family, friends and associates. Too often has this been forgotten, with the tragic result that the individual believer makes little progress in effective Christian living. Although we may not agree with many of the emphases in Horace Bushnell's presentation of the gospel, he certainly sounded the trumpet clearly in his day, when he wrote on this matter in *Christian Nurture* in these words, "It becomes a question of great moment, as connected with the doctrine established, whether it is the design of the Christian scheme to take possession of the organic laws of the family, and wield them as instruments, in any sense, of a regenerative purpose? And here we are met by the broad principle, that Christianity endeavors to make every object, favor, and relation, an instrument of righteousness, according to its original design."[1]

Much easier is it to speak of spiritual matters with only one or two than in the presence of a whole family. But why should this be so? Are we to conclude that the profession of many of our Reformed people is so often contradicted by their daily conduct, that they are compelled to silence about such important matters, when in the presence of those with whom they live daily?

Many times Reformed family visitation has been caricatured. The picture too often drawn is that of a large family, all properly scrubbed and dressed, patiently waiting for the visit which has been previously announced to the whole congregation. The children have been instructed to say as little as possible, preferably limiting their answers to "yes" and "no." As footsteps are heard without, the tension mounts and almost reaches the breaking-point when the

[1]Bushnell: *Christian Nurture,* p. 110, 111.

elders enter the room. Thereupon a few pleasantries are exchanged about work and weather, but all know that the dread questioning about spiritual matters will soon begin. First the father is interrogated at length, then the mother, and finally the children from the oldest to the youngest. What a sigh of relief, when prayer has been offered and the brethren depart! For another year life in the family, having successfully weathered another crisis in its routine, can resume its usual course. And if the dread ordeal has been survived without the betrayal of too much on the part of any member of the family, all are happy.

Without endeavoring to argue that family visitation never answers to the above picture, we dare affirm that this is by no means the general situation. If it were, we would do well to lament the fearful plight of a church which had sunk to such low spiritual depths.

If both elders and members would remember the real purpose of these official calls, family visitation would seldom if ever seem like an unpleasant ordeal. Since Christ through His officers supervises the lives of the members of His church, we may confidently expect from the elders the manifestation of the sympathetic spirit of our heavenly Highpriest who "was in all points tempted like as we are, yet without sin." They come not to find fault but rather to comfort and encourage, in order that the Lord's people may be strengthened in their faith and deepened in their love for the Savior and the saints. If believers are thus to be benefited, they should manifest the same sincerity and frankness which ought to characterize their prayers to God for help and strength.

Dare we, then, discuss the conditions and needs of spiritual life in the presence of other members of the family? Surely if there is a striving to manifest the spirit of Christ, this will present no difficulties. Here the words of Paul to the Corinthian church are much to the point. "Love suffereth long, and is kind; love envieth not; love vaunted not itself, is not puffed up, doth not behave itself unseemly, seeketh not its own, is not provoked, taketh not account of evil; rejoiceth not in unrighteousness, but rejoiceth in the truth; beareth all things, believeth all things, hopeth all things, endureth all things."[1]

It is true that there will be matters demanding utmost privacy. These may never be discussed at family visitation but definitely re-

[1]I Corinthians 13:4-7.

quire consideration at another time. However, if we bear in mind that basically all Christians have the same spiritual struggles, it is both proper and helpful to discuss them with each other. From the experiences of the parents the children may learn much. There will result a far better understanding of each other's failings and an earnest desire to help each other in love which will draw all the members of the family together. The responsibilities of children towards parents and of parents towards children will be seen and appreciated more clearly. And in this way the Christian family will become one of the most influential factors in the spiritual development of believers, old and young alike.

What hampers this work most is false modesty on the part of all. It is often engendered by a wrong conception that family visitation attains its goal, when all the members can successfully persuade the elders that they are very good Christians. Even as Christ came not to save the righteous but to call sinners to repentance, so the elders who come in the name of Christ can be of no help to those who feel no need. Only those who know the power of indwelling sin, are sincerely repentant of their sins, turn daily to Christ, and earnestly resolve to live for Him will experience a rich blessing through the exhortation, admonition and encouragement of the servants of Christ. Then this practice which has stood the test of history will prove spiritually fruitful for years to come.

THE REQUISITES FOR FAMILY VISITATION

"We have said that love to Christ does not impose on all His disciples the duty of a shepherd; showing itself rather in by far the larger number in simply hearing the shepherd's voice and following him, and generally in a willingness to be guided by those who are wiser than themselves. We must add, that all who are animated by the spirit of love to the Redeemer, will be either shepherds or sheep, actively useful in caring for the souls of others, or thankfully using the provision made for the care of their own souls."

A. B. BRUCE: THE TRAINING OF THE TWELVE.

In the stirring days of Oliver Cromwell there was great concern on the part of many for the reformation of Christ's church in England. During those years the highly esteemed pastor and preacher Richard Baxter published his work on *The Reformed Pastor* which to this very day is still an invaluable guide for those who have the oversight of the flock of the Savior.

"We must have a special eye upon families," so he wrote, "to see that they are well ordered, and the duties of each relation performed. The life of religion, and the welfare and glory of both the Church and the State, depend much upon family government and duty. If we suffer the neglect of this, we shall undo all. What are we like to do ourselves to the reforming of a congregation, if all the work be cast on us alone; and masters of families neglect that necessary duty of their own, by which they are bound to help us? If any good be begun by the ministry in any soul, a careless, prayerless, worldly family is like to stifle it, or very much hinder it; whereas, if you could but get the rulers of families to do their duty, to take up the work where you left it, and help it on, what abundance of good might be done! I beseech you, therefore, if you desire the reformation and welfare of your people, do all you can to promote family religion."[1]

Much of the effectiveness of this type of work, however, will depend upon the manner in which it is accomplished. Therefore we do well to consider some of the basic requisites for family visitation. These may be reduced to three which are the most comprehensive and important. If any congregation is to derive spiritual benefit

[1]Baxter: *The Reformed Pastor*, p. 91.

from it, the work must be done *officially, regularly* and *with due regard for its purpose.*

The Official Character of This Work

Although we have already touched on the official nature of this work, it requires some broader and more detailed consideration now.

The Reformed churches, in contrast to many other Protestant denominations, have always esteemed the offices highly. Although they reacted vigorously against the usurpation of power of which the Romish hierarchy had made itself guilty during the centuries immediately preceding the Reformation, they refused to fall into the opposite extreme. In fact, the Reformed fathers saw much more clearly than the Roman Catholic church authorities the value and use of the New Testament offices.

By a careful study of the several parts of the New Testament these leaders saw that the good government of the church of Christ required three types of officers — the ministers of the Word, the elders and the deacons. Each in its own way represented some aspect of the triple office of the Savior, who as Head of His church remained the final seat of all authority and the source of all power in the life of the congregations.

This power which He delegated to His representatives was defined as regulative and spiritual. Although the officers were clothed with authority, this was not inherent in their persons, and therefore they were to regard themselves as shepherds and servants of the flock of Christ. As a result abuses of power could not creep into the church easily, if it was aware of and safeguarded its right. Abraham Kuyper in his work on *Calvinism* remarks on this matter as follows: "This government, like the church itself, originates in heaven, in Christ. He most effectually rules, governs His church by means of the Holy Spirit, by whom He works in His members. Therefore all being equal under Him, there can be no distinctions of rank among believers; there are only ministers, who serve, lead and regulate; a thoroughly Presbyterian form of government; the Church power descending directly from Christ Himself, into the congregation, concentrated from the congregation in the ministers, and by them being administered unto the brethren. So the sovereignty of Christ remains absolutely monarchical, but the government of the Church on earth becomes democratic to its bones and marrow . . ."[1]

[1]Kuyper: *Calvinism*, p. 77.

This idea of the officers as pastors who serve the flock is thoroughly Scriptural. However, it was felt at once that certain distinctions had to be made for the sake of good order. When speaking of pastors, the Reformed fathers used the term in two ways. First of all, they might use the word in a more restricted sense, when they designated the work of the ministers of the Word to whom fell the task of preaching and teaching the Word. But they could also speak of it in a broader sense and thus hold that all spiritual work by the officers is pastoral in its nature. All three offices are bound to the Word, and the purpose of each is to show the members how to conduct themselves as sheep and lambs of the flock.

Thus the work of the elders, too, is definitely pastoral. The power which is delegated to them is for the purpose of ministering to the spiritual needs of the people.

This ordinary office in the New Testament church, in distinction from the work of the apostles, prophets and evangelists, was of a permanent nature. Elders were to be appointed in all the churches, in order that the work of the gospel might go forward even when the apostles and their helpers fell away. These men were called by two names: presbyters or elders, and bishops or overseers. Both terms are self-explanatory. The first refers chiefly to the dignity with which the office was clothed, and the second to the specific work which was enjoined upon those who were called to it. These men were to take heed to the whole flock of the Lord, carefully supervising both the doctrine and conduct of all the members. In order that this might be done adequately, it was deemed necessary by the Reformed churches at the very beginning of their history to visit the members in their homes at stated times. By a frank and free discussion of the nature and development of spiritual life with the members, the elders could instruct and comfort and admonish as need required.

Indeed, it was recognized cheerfully that upon many other occasions spiritual life could be discussed profitably. The members by virtue of the office of all believers were to help and comfort and admonish each other. Likewise, both minister and elders could upon special occasions visit the members for the same purpose. Even in the execution of their tasks the deacons were to remember the pastoral nature of their calling. However, none of these instances could relieve the elders of their responsibility. They, as watchmen upon the walls of Zion and shepherds of the saints, were to know the needs of all and help them from time to time.

When therefore the elders come into the homes of the members, they come in the name of their Exalted Savior. Instead of seeing only the persons of the elders, the members should recognize the presence of their Savior and Lord in the ministrations of men.

It may be asked, What is the place of the minister of the Word in family visitation? This question is proper, especially in view of the fact that in many churches most of this work is expected of him. Too often many of our members labor under the misconception that the office of the minister is higher in rank than that of the elders and deacons. Anyone who carefully studies the New Testament texts which refer to the offices will be able to point out the fallacy of this idea at once. Although his office differs from the other two in kind, it is in no way inherently superior. Thus when he accompanies an elder at family visitation, he too comes as a ruling elder of the church.

It has generally been recognized in the Reformed churches that the minister of the Word labors in a double capacity. He has two offices which he must discharge. Not only is he to labor in the official teaching of the Word, but he is also appointed to assist the other elders in the ruling of the church. This is plain from the *Form for the Ordination of the Ministers of God's Word,* where his several duties are outlined in great detail. There we read, "Fourth: the task of the ministers of the Word is with the elders to keep the Church of God in good discipline, and to govern it in such a manner as the Lord has ordained; for Christ, having spoken of the Christian discipline, says to His apostles: Whatsoever thou shalt bind on earth shall be bound in heaven (Matt. 16:19). And Paul would have the ministers know how to rule their own house, since otherwise they can neither provide for nor rule the Church of God. This is the reason why in Scripture the pastors are also called stewards of God and bishops, that is, overseers and watchmen; for they have the oversight of the house of God, wherein they abide, to the end that there everything may be transacted with good order and decency; and that they may open and shut, with the keys of the kingdom of heaven committed to them, according to the charge given them by God."

Thus the members of the consistory, when calling upon the families to discharge their office of supervising the flock, should be regarded with honor. They come in the name of Christ, and for the purpose of ministering to the needs of His people. Their call should be announced beforehand, in order that the whole family may be present. When we feel the need of medical or legal aid, we do not hesitate to make and keep appointments with physicians, dentists and lawyers. Can it then be considered improper that official appointments are made for this spiritual work? Only in so far as the work is properly respected can it be effective in the life of the church.

The Need of Regularity in the Work

Another requisite for the proper conducting of family visitation is regularity. During past years much has been said and written about its frequency. In discussing the matter we ought to guard against two dangers. It may be carried on so infrequently and irregularly, that the membership of the church loses sight of its spiritual nature and necessity entirely, with the tragic result that family visitation degenerates into a social call. However, it may also be done so often that the elders and members fall into meaningless repetition.

It is very significant that already at the first broader assembly of the Reformed churches of the Netherlands (Convent of Wezel in 1568) this question was discussed, and as a result it was decided that all the families of the churches should be visited by the elders once a week. The decision is not at all strange, when we consider the need of those days. At this assembly the first Church Order by which the congregations were to govern themselves was drawn up. Only shortly before many of the members had left the Roman Catholic church, where weekly confession to the priest was a general practice. Moreover, many of these new members were quite ignorant of the rule of the gospel. Family visitation, then, provided the elders with a wonderful opportunity for instructing and admonishing the members. Without a doubt, where this was done properly, rich spiritual blessings accrued to the churches. Some time later the present reading of Article 23 of our Church Order was drawn up, in which it was stipulated that these official visits should be made to all the members "before and after the Lord's Supper, as time and circumstances may demand."

All are agreed that it is no longer necessary to conduct this work weekly among the whole congregation. Not only would this be practically impossible in all of our churches, but both members and elders would fall into endless repetition after a few times. Actual supervision of the members does not require knowledge of all the details of individual spiritual life. On this basis the Reformed churches have as a general principle repudiated the practice of inquiring into all the details of the believer's relation to God and his fellow-men, as was so often done in the Roman Catholic confessional. The church as the mother of the faithful is required to assist with counsel and comfort instead of lording it over the lives of her members.

With these facts in mind we can understand why the churches have adopted the custom of conducting family visitation in such a way that all are contacted at least once a year. This ought to be considered a minimum requirement. If longer periods are allowed to lapse between the official visits, there is great danger of ineffectiveness. The confidence of the members in their officers will greatly suffer, and the elders on their side can hardly claim to know the needs of the congregation as a whole, if two or three years expire between visits. That large congregations because of their size make it extremely difficult to conduct the work systematically each year has often been advanced as an excuse for not adhering to the custom of annual visitation. However, if both ministers and elders are convinced of the importance and necessity of the work, they will take the necessary time. It is significant that often elders in the large congregations are fully as conscientious about this part of their calling as those in smaller churches. Indeed, the minister in a congregation of more than two hundred families cannot possibly visit every family annually without neglecting some other part of his work. Yet, if we but remember that this is part of his work as ruling elder rather than as minister of the Word, we will realize that he is not required to do much more of this work than the other elders in the consistory. And should the complaint be heard that family visitation is effective only when the minister calls on the members, the solution to this problem lies not in the direction of visiting the congregation less frequently (say, only once in two or three years in order that the minister may be present at every visit) but rather in the direction of training our eldership for its own peculiar work.

Keeping Its Purpose in Mind

One other requisite for family visitation demands our attention. The work, if to be done effectively, must be conducted purposefully. The officers should be able to give a clear account of their calling, when they visit the families, and thus give direction to the conversation in which they engage the members.

We have reacted strongly against what has often, but improperly, been called the "inquisitorial" method of family visitation. By this is understood the method of direct questioning in order to stimulate conversation on spiritual matters. It cannot be denied that the elders are often rather shy about directing such questions and prefer to allow the conversation to take whatever course it will. As a result some of the most important matters are conveniently dodged.

In opposing such a desultory way of carrying on the work let no one think that we are defending those individuals (and there have been such!) who because of the dignity of their eldership have deemed it their prerogative to inquire into every secret of the believer's life. Those who so "lord it over the flock" forget that they are servants for Christ's sake.

However, we may not forget that the elders are clothed with spiritual authority. It is therefore their duty to see to it that spiritual matters are discussed at family visitation. And should there be those who try to steer the conversation, whether consciously or unconsciously, in another direction, the elders must remind themselves and the members of the purpose of their call. Of course, this must be done as unobtrusively and charitably as possible. Only when it is apparent that the individual who is being visited deliberately refuses to speak about his relation to God and his fellowmen should he be rebuked, and even then in the spirit of love and kindness.

How can we do justice to the demand of purposeful family visitation? Because we resent the use of any stereotyped set of questions, it is not easy to answer this question. Spiritual life is organic and must always be approached with this knowledge in mind. It is therefore so dangerous to classify the members into groups depending upon the level of spirituality. As in the realm of nature no two snowflakes are alike, so in the kingdom of grace we find an infinite variety among the believers. Yet a few general remarks are not out of place here.

First of all, we should lament the fact that family visitation too often has degenerated to mere routine in our churches. Once a year all the members must be visited. Thus long lists of calls are prepared in advance. The more calls made in one evening, the sooner the work is finished. Thus there is danger that the work loses all spontaneity and naturalness. Those who do the calling should remember that every visit is a challenge. As believers differ from each other, their needs and wants will vary. It is the business of the elders to know and understand these needs, as well as the gospel of Christ which alone can satisfy the requirements of the spiritual life of His people.

Thus, too, it is essential that the elders themselves be spiritually equipped for their work. This cannot be done without prayer and study. To fulfil this part of their calling they must enjoy the constant guidance of God's Spirit. Only when consciously and completely leaning upon Him will they receive the words which they are to bring to the people.

Whenever possible, the elders ought to know the particular needs of the families which they are to visit. Thus it is profitable that the consistory (in strictest confidence, of course, and prompted only by the purest motives) discuss the spiritual condition of the several families in so far as these are known to the elders. This allows for noting the changes which take place, whether for good or ill.

But above all both elders and people must be constantly reminded of the goal of the work — the spiritual equipment of the congregation to serve God in singleness of heart. Many opportunities for doing this will present themselves during the year. In public worship and catechetical classes remarks on the nature and purpose of the work are often in place. An announcement from the pulpit or in the bulletin at the time family visitation is carried on, will often prove effective. The more clearly the purpose is understood by all, the easier it will be to cherish high hopes that also this arduous spiritual labor will benefit consistory and congregation alike.

OBJECTIONS TO FAMILY VISITATION

"We admit, therefore, that ecclesiastical pastors are to be heard just like Christ Himself, but they must be pastors who execute the office entrusted to them. And this office, we maintain, is not presumptuously to introduce whatever their own pleasure has rashly devised, but religiously and in good faith to deliver the oracles which they have received at the mouth of the Lord. For within these boundaries Christ confined the reverence which he required to be paid to the Apostles; nor does Peter (I Pet. iv:11) either claim for himself or allow to others anything more than that, as often as they speak among the faithful, they speak as from the mouth of the Lord."

JOHN CALVIN: REPLY TO CARDINAL SADOLET.

"Saints, by profession, are bound to maintain an holy fellowship and communion in the worship of God, and in performing such other spiritual services as tend to their mutual edification . . ."

WESTMINSTER CONFESSION OF FAITH
Chapter XXVI, 2.

To anyone who has followed our discussion to this point, it will be apparent that some careful attention must still be given to the many objections which are raised against the practice of family visitation, if the practice is to profit the churches in the years to come.

We have with us those who claim that in spite of all the good features of this venerable practice, the insurmountable difficulties are so many, that we do best to dispense with it at once and perhaps substitute some other type of spiritual care.

In dealing with the difficulties we ought to bear in mind that it is not necessary to give more than a passing glance to those who refuse to be convinced. Perhaps there are some also in our churches who have closed their minds to all arguments in favor of this official church care of the families. These, however, are not motivated by genuine love for the church of Christ and may be dismissed together with all their protestations without more ado.

But others who are sincere in raising objections are entitled to a fair hearing.

In the main the objections are of two kinds. First of all, there are some who maintain the principle that ideally in the Reformed churches there should be no supervision of the membership by those in authority, since all believers are equal in rank before Christ and

God in the New Testament church. Others point out the many practical difficulties which arise wherever this custom is followed and argue that it would be beneficial to spiritual life to dispense with it. In this section we would look into the arguments which the opponents of family visitation have raised.

A Poor Substitute for the Confessional

Occasionally we will still hear individuals make the claim that family visitation, as we know it, should have no place in the churches, because it is at very best but a poor substitute for the Roman Catholic confessional.

On the surface this argument seems to have the support of history, for Calvin did institute the practice in the churches of Geneva after the confessional was rejected. In many respects there are striking similarities between the two forms of membership supervision. Both are deeply concerned with the spiritual life of the believer and proceed on the assumption that the church through her officers has the divinely-given duty of watching for the souls of those entrusted to her care.

A more careful scrutiny of the matter, however, will prove that this similarity is only superficial. Calvin never suggested that it was a substitute for the confessional in any way. There were very positive Scriptural objections to the Romish confessional which made its rejection imperative. Thus family visitation was only part of the broader positive reformatory ideal of bringing the life of the church closer to the New Testament pattern.

Family visitation should not be confused with personal work among the members required by the consistory. This last has a province all its own. Time and again it will be necessary for the elders to call upon individual members of the congregation, in order that they may be strengthened in the faith and warned against the ways of sin. We need only mention that family visitation in the Reformed churches has never displaced the visitation of the sick, the spiritually distressed and the wayward.

What the Bible teaches plainly is the close relation between nature and grace. When bestowing His salvation, God does not take us out of this present world. Neither do we become "new creatures" in this sense that the social relationships found among all men can be ignored by us. Therefore it is a fallacy to suppose that the spiritual problems of the believer can be considered in isolation.

The fact that we have been created as social beings for whom it is not good to live alone comes to its fullest and richest expression in our relation to the families. Our whole life consists of relationship — to God, ourselves, our families, our neighbors, our fellowmen in general. As a result we cannot live out our faith in a vacuum. The spiritual life controlled by love to God and His Word can never be practiced solely in the recesses of our hearts. In family visitation this truth becomes a guiding principle for the spiritual labors of the elders. Our religious life is organically related to all that we think and speak and do, and this is not only of the greatest consequence to our families with whom we live most intimately but can also be properly understood and evaluated only when considered in this light.

Thus Reformed family visitation differs radically from the practice of the confessional. It alone can do justice to the organic character of human life.

Even more, we reject the whole Romish system of penance which is intimately bound up with the practice of auricular confession. For it there is no place in our churches. Thus the elders may never pry into the recesses of the heart, in a vain endeavor to bring secret sins to light. By emphasizing so strongly the priesthood of all believers the Reformed churches reject the notion that the visible church is the necessary mediatrix between God and the soul. What we possess in the type of spiritual care of the members of the church is not a poor substitute for the confessional but a practice which is in principle far different from anything known to the Roman Catholic church and infinitely superior to it.

A Denial of the Equality of All Believers

Others insist that family visitation ought to be discarded, because it conflicts with the democratic ideal of the equality of all members before God. These claim that no group in the church ought to possess the right of ruling the others.

Now if we are at all aware of the confusion which characterizes Protestant thinking today, we will realize at once that this objection can only be raised by those who either consciously or unconsciously have rejected the Reformed theory of the church of Christ. It was among the Anabaptists of the days of the Reformation that such claims for the absolute equality of all believers were made.

Reformed Christians indeed believe strongly that in the sight of Almighty God all men are equal and therefore have the right to be treated alike. God is no respecter of persons; hence rich and poor, bond and free, learned and ignorant stand alike under the condemnation of the law by nature and can receive salvation only by sovereign grace. However, this is something far different from the Anabaptist insistence on equality which repudiates authority in the visible church.

Although there is a basic equality of person in the sight of God, there is no equality of function or calling. The Scriptures plainly teach that God Himself makes distinctions for the sake of the good order and the edification of His people in the church. "And He gave some to be apostles; and some, prophets; and some, pastors and teachers, for the perfecting of the saints, for the building up of the body of Christ . . ."[1] Likewise are the faithful enjoined to "submit yourselves unto the elder. Yea, all of you, be subject one to another, and be clothed with humility."[2] Still stronger is the language used by the writer of the epistle to the Hebrews, "Obey them that have the rule over you, and submit yourselves; for they watch for your souls, as they that must give account, that they may do it with joy, and not with grief; for that is not profitable for you."[3]

From these passages it must appear that government in the churches is necessary. For our spiritual welfare God has entrusted the rule to men of good repute who have been chosen in the lawful way by the members themselves. Though in no way enjoying any personal preeminence, they are charged with the rule of the congregation. And since it is a ministry or spiritual service, it may never lead to tyranny. To prevent such a calamity there are always several in office, so that each elder in turn must submit himself to the government of the rest.

Instead of being contrary to the New Testament teaching of the spiritual equality of the believers, the Reformed practice of family visitation is in complete harmony with its insistence that officers have been appointed for the strengthening of the body of Christ in the true faith and godliness. Without such official supervision

[1]Ephesians 4:11, 12.
[2]I Peter 5:5.
[3]Hebrews 13:17.

grievous heresies and wicked practices would soon overwhelm the church in this present evil world and threaten her with total extinction.

A Legalistic Conception of Spiritual Life

At times the objection is raised that family visitation roots in a legalistic conception of spiritual life and the relation of the officers of the church to her members. On these grounds it should then be refused a place of honor in our church life.

By legalism is meant the theory that spiritual life can be reduced to external compliance with a set of rules or principles adopted to regulate the conduct of God's people. On this basis the elders would act in the capacity of spiritual police with the duty of enforcing the laws. If the laws are obeyed, they may conclude that all is well. Such a policy of enforcing obedience, so the objectors counter, robs the Christian of his New Testament liberty in Christ and hinders rather than promotes true spirituality. On this basis they would not hesitate to compare family visitation with the medieval inquisition which insisted on strict conformity in all matters religious and arrogated to itself the right to judge the heart.

It need hardly be said that this representation rests entirely upon a misunderstanding of the nature and purpose of family visitation. The proper supervision of the members, as has been demonstrated before, must not degenerate into a system of policing and spying on the congregation.

Yet it ought to be added that the tendency of our modern age is revolutionary. There is little respect for law and government. The individual, as a result of the insidious influence of much of modern philosophy, regards himself as the final authority in spiritual matters. He claims for himself the inherent right of deciding how and when and where he shall serve God and his fellow-men. Should such fallacious theories become wide-spread in the church, its spiritual life would suffer appreciably. All insistence upon law is not *per se* legalism by any means. Would that we had more regard for the authority with which Christ promulgates His laws in the church!

Instead of being an inquisition, family visitation is a discussion of spiritual life and its problems, to be conducted in such a way that both elders and members of the church profit thereby. Because the work is spiritual and positive in character, aiming at the edification of the believers, it requires the whole-hearted cooperation of those who are visited. If at any time this objection can be levelled against the present practice with any degree of justification (a possibility which may never be ignored!), it ought to be regarded not as an objection to family visitation as such but rather to the way in which it is conducted by certain individuals.

A Fruitless Work Because of Its Formal Character

An objection of a somewhat different color is that this work is necessarily fruitless, because of its formal approach to spiritual life.

Voices are raised in protest occasionally against the formal character of this work. They argue that since the announcement of the day and hour of the call is made, with the result that all the members of the family are adequately prepared, no true judgment can be made of the spiritual condition of the people under those circumstances. A conscious effort is made by every individual to present himself in the best light. All the questions are answered most cautiously. When the elders leave after an hour, they carry with them an impression of the family which is far from being a true reflection of what they really are.

Again, this is not an objection to the principle of family visitation at all, but rather to the way in which it may be conducted. That there will always be certain families who try consciously to present such an unreal picture of their spiritual condition can hardly be doubted. Yet would we dare claim that this is true of the majority in our churches? Has not every minister and elder in seriously attempting to perform this work effectively been gratified upon many occasions with the unaffected and frank response on the part of many of the people? That we do not see our people at their worst ought to occasion no surprise. However, that they would definitely try to deceive the officers of Christ's church by posing as better than they really are can be maintained only by the most thorough-going pessimist. And should this situation obtain among a sizeable number of members, it can be overcome by regularly and patiently explaining to the people the true spiritual purpose of the visits which are made.

An Unwelcome and Unappreciated Work

But our church members, so some would claim, do not like family visitation at all; they tolerate it simply because it has been the rule for so many years and the consistory still insists on it. If the members of the congregation were permitted to decide on the matter, the vote in favor of its abolishment would be overwhelming.

Now this objection is a very serious one, if it can be substantiated with facts. It would prove that the spiritual life of the congregations has sunk to a new low, both because the members are unwilling or unable to discuss spiritual matters and because the elders have not learned the art of conducting this part of their calling properly and profitably.

We are convinced that this is a totally inaccurate picture of the church today. That there are some who do not appreciate these visits at all need not surprise anyone. If the spiritual life of the believer reveals no depth, he will feel very uncomfortable indeed, when these matters are considered and he finds himself with little or nothing to say. Also those who have hardened themselves in sinful practices of one kind or another will resent any supposed interference in their lives by the elders on the fallacious ground that they have the right to live as they please.

Let us remember that such unpleasant and unspiritual conditions in the church argue strongly in favor of family visitation rather than against it. When conducted in the spirit of Christ, be it with weakness and imperfection, most believers will soon learn to appreciate this work deeply, convinced that this spiritual counsel and comfort is administered in the name of the Savior Himself.

If for one reason or another a large element in the congregation continues to resent this aspect of pastoral work, the consistory should nevertheless patiently and lovingly bear with such individuals and persevere in instruction and admonition, knowing that the appreciation of men is never the standard by which we are to judge the value or effectiveness of a Christian ministry. Often the most necessary labors in life are the least appreciated.

An Unnecessary Work in a Normal Church

When all is said and done, there will still be individuals who, while admitting many of the principles which underlie this work, hold that it is unnecessary in a congregation where spiritual life is normal.

To reinforce their contention they will argue that in the days of Calvin and shortly thereafter, it was absolutely essential to visit the families, because so many of the members of the Reformed churches at that time had but recently left the Roman Catholic fold and were still strangers to most of the practices of the true religion. Therefore they admit that the Convent of Wezel (1568) did right in instituting family visitation. However, with centuries of Reformed teaching and tradition behind us and with all the excellent facilities which we enjoy for the development of spiritual life such as Christian homes and schools and churches, it is sheer waste of time and effort to visit our families annually.

Granting for a moment that spiritual life in many of our churches is rather normal, should we not add immediately that family visitation would still be necessary, in order that the elders may be reasonably assured of this healthy condition? How else, if this practice were discarded, would the supervisors of the church be able to discharge their duty and give a good account of themselves and their work to Christ who is the Head of His church? Is not the preventative work which is performed every time a visit is made worth all the time and effort expended? Surely no one can with any show of reason deny these facts.

But more than this, we ought to consider seriously the question of what constitutes normal spirituality in the church. Just what do those who object to family visitation mean by that phrase? Is it ever possible to find "normal" spirituality in this abnormal world, so full of sin and temptation on every hand? Spiritual life consists of our religious fellowship with God through Jesus Christ by the operation of His Holy Spirit. And nothing less than perfection may be considered normal, since it involves our relation to the infinitely perfect and holy Covenant God and prepares us in this life for an eternity of unbroken and indescribably blessed fellowship with Him.

Here we find so many ailments and diseases which constantly undermine and seek to destroy that blessed covenant relation. The eye of our faith is often dimmed by both the trials and pleasures of this life. The desire of the heart to serve the Lord with undivided affection is not nearly so fervent as it should be. Instead of an unhampered growth in the grace and the knowledge of the Lord Jesus Christ, we must often complain of spiritual coldness and uncertainty resulting from our apathy to and neglect of the things of the Spirit of God. And since such disturbing factors impinge upon our lives not once or twice but are a constant source of danger and discouragement on the way of sanctification, we should become increasingly convinced of our need of instruction and encouragement in this life.

This is, of course, first of all worked in our hearts by the preaching of the holy gospel and the administration of the sacraments. Yet who can deny that it is also admirably reinforced by the personal contacts made by the elders at the time of family visitation? In a word, spiritual life can never be said to be "normal" in the true sense of the word as long as we are in this life. For that blessing we must wait for the dawning of the eternal day, when we shall serve God perfectly and shall be satisfied with beholding His face forever. Until then the eldership in its spiritual work should help the believers grow unto full salvation.

A Disregard of the Needs of the Individual

Yet one more argument against the practice of family visitation should be considered at this time. It is presented perhaps oftener than any other today. Modern psychology has reminded us of the inestimable benefits of personal discussion with those who are spiritually distressed. But, so the argument runs, no one feels free to discuss his individual problems in the presence of the other members of the family.

There is to be sure much truth in this presentation of the case. Still more if we suppose that these visits should be patterned after the policy of the Roman Catholic confessional, they will never attain their goal. In spiritual life there is much which we confess only to God and can occasionally reveal only to some intimate and trusted friend. To uncover these hidden thoughts and troubles of the heart and discuss them in the presence of others violates the dignity of human personality.

But let us remember that this is not the purpose of these visits, any more than it can be the aim of the gospel preaching to make a direct application to all the needs of the members of the congregation. Because family visitation offers a wonderful opportunity for considering the needs and nature of spiritual life from time to time, it will stimulate the members to examine their lives in the light of God's Word and regulate them accordingly. At the time of preaching we are taught to make the application of God's truth to our own lives. The same holds true of family visitation. Furthermore, when this work is carried on in the spirit of Christian sympathy and helpfulness, confidence in the elders is awakened in the hearts of the members. Then those individuals who still have perplexing problems which ought not and cannot be revealed in the presence of all will meet one of the elders privately for counsel and help.

We should never forget that family visitation may and often must be supplemented with calls of a more personal character. Such follow-up work yields rich and satisfying results for all concerned. The good undershepherd will learn to know his sheep better as he meets them regularly and will be prepared to help them when occasion requires. But this can hardly be successfully realized, unless the ground-work of mutual trust and respect has been laid. For this last no time is so propitious as that of the annual visit to all the families of the church.

THE VALUE OF FAMILY VISITATION

"We look in upon the Christian family, where everything is on a footing of religion, and we see them around their own quiet hearth and table, away from the great public world and its strifes, with a priest of their own to lead them. They are knit together in ties of love that make them one; even as they are fed and clothed out of the same fund, interested in the same possessions, partakers in the same successes and losses, suffering together in the same sorrows, animated each by hopes that respect the future benefit of all. Into such a circle and scene it is that religion comes, each day, to obtain a grace of well-doing for the day . . . It leads in the day, as dawn leads in the morning. It blends a heavenly gratitude with the joys of the table; it breathes a cheerful sense of God into all the works and tempers of the house; it softens the pillow for rest when the day is done. And so the religion of the house is life itself, the life of life; and having always been observed, it becomes an integral part even of existence, leaving no feeling that, in a proper family it could ever have been otherwise."

HORACE BUSHNELL: CHRISTIAN NURTURE.

In spite of all the objections which have been raised against the practice of family visitation as we have come to know and love it in our churches, so much spiritual value inheres in the work if conducted properly that we greatly impoverish ourselves by either carrying it on carelessly or neglecting it altogether.

Spiritual blessings, we are convinced, will accrue not only to the members of the church but quite as much to the consistory which zealously seeks to perform this part of its calling.

For the Eldership

(1) The first benefit for the elders which ought to be mentioned is that diligent pursuance of this practice will enable them to know the spiritual condition of the flock over which the Lord has placed them.

Many experienced elders will cheerfully witness to the truth of that statement. Especially in our larger congregations where members come and go regularly there is a danger that only the pastor knows who belongs. And since he may be called to another field of labor at any time, it is essential to the well-being of the church that the elders are as thoroughly acquainted with the needs of the people as possible. They will in periods of vacancy be compelled to carry on many of the labors which otherwise devolve upon the minister of the gospel. How much easier it is to visit the sick and call on the delinquents, when the members of the consistory are acquainted with the conditions in the family beforehand. Many situations which else would be puzzling often present no problem at all, when one understands the background of the case. The more the elders know the spiritual level of the members, the better able they will be to give wise Christian counsel. And this will contribute in no small way to help them present the challenge of their church intelligently to their next pastor.

(2) By conducting the work prayerfully and regularly the members of the consistory will also know whether or not the believers over whom they have been placed make spiritual progress by using the means of grace. Those who superintend the flock must not only know whether the members are diligent in church attendance but also whether they receive spiritual blessings.

Of course, this does not mean that minister and elders must make it their policy to cater to the tastes of the people. Such an attempt is beneath the spiritual dignity of the officers of Christ's church. Many people in Jesus' day also followed Him solely for the loaves and the fishes and forsook Him when His words seemed hard and mysterious. The rule may well be applied here that what people do not like is often just what they need.

Yet it must be a matter of deepest concern to consecrated officebearers whether or not the Word of God challenges their lives and influences them for good. This knowledge which may best be gleaned at family visitation should be frankly and freely discussed in the spirit of Christian brotherliness and concern for the advancement of the gospel cause at the meetings of the consistory.

(3) These visits likewise give the elders a much-needed opportunity for engaging in preventative work, with the result that instances of glaring defection from the rule of gospel become more infrequent among the people of God. An ounce of prevention in spiritual work is worth a pound of cure any time. Family visitation affords an opportunity not to be despised, of pointing out the weakness of the flesh and of encouraging Christians to "put on the new man, that after God hath been created in righteousness and holiness of truth."[1]

This is quite different from trying to frighten people into a life of godliness. Such an attempt would fail miserably. True growth in grace is always the result of an internal compulsion worked in the

[1]Ephesians 4:24.

heart by the Spirit of God. However, by means of words of wisdom and kindness such spiritual desires, which for a time may seem to lie quite dormant in the heart, may be fanned into a flame which will burn purely and brightly to God's glory and the good name of the church of Christ.

(4) We should not forget that such visits also stimulate the spiritual unity of believers.

How easy it is to forget in our days of rank individualism that we are members of the body of Christ, and though our callings differ, we are all given to each other for the purpose of mutual edification! Paul writes to the believers at Corinth, "So also ye, since ye are zealous of spiritual gifts, seek that ye may abound unto the edifying of the church."[1]

Many minor difficulties and misunderstandings have been removed in congregations where the elders were faithful in the execution of their holy office. Long before such problems become ripe for consistorial action, they can be nipped in the bud and thus prevent much unpleasantness and rancor. So often when discipline must be applied, the case in hand defies a happy solution. When at the time of family visitation it becomes apparent that members live at odds with each other, the elders can point to the rule of Matthew 18 before the matter assumes serious proportions. At such a time the lofty ideal of living together as brethren and sisters of the spiritual family of God can be appropriately held up, and with the unfailing help of the Holy Spirit who alone applies the Word effectually stumblingblocks will be removed.

(5) Finally this custom enables the elders to demonstrate in a practical way the spirit of Christian love and helpfulness.

The rule which they bear has been given for the purpose of ministering to each other. Those called to the office should remember the example which our Saviour gave His disciples at the Last Supper, when after the foot-washing He said, "Know ye what I have done to you? Ye call me, Teacher, and Lord: and ye say well; for so I am. If I then, the Lord and the Teacher, have washed your feet, ye also ought to wash one another's feet. For I have given you an example, that ye should do as I have done to you. Verily, verily, I say unto you, A servant is not greater than his lord; neither one that is sent than he that sent him. If ye know these things, blessed are ye if ye

[1] I Corinthians 14:12.

do them."[1] Striving to fulfill the law so clearly presented here will effectively banish from the minds and hearts of all elders any spirit of censoriousness and self-righteousness. In the discharge of their spiritual functions they will remember to mirror the office of the Savior who Himself was the Great Shepherd of the sheep.

For the Congregation

Not only do the elders derive much benefit from this work, but the believing church also profits much. They will experience that by means of it they are built up in faith and increased in love.

(1) First of all, as members of the living church they will see more clearly the value of discussing matters pertaining to spiritual life.

In our age, in which leisure is at a premium and the things of the Spirit are constantly clouded over by earthly and material interests, it is so necessary to emphasize this. Many find it difficult to speak to each other about these matters of supreme importance. Not only is there great reluctance to discuss spiritual problems and difficulties which are quite common to all, but most members testify very little to the joy of salvation which should be their portion. We have apparently lost sight of the necessity of edifying one another. This duty we too often leave entirely to the minister when preaching the Word.

Even a cursory and superficial reading of the New Testament will prove that such is the duty of all the members. Perhaps one of the chief reasons why many have no well-defined conception of what truly constitutes Christian living as fellowship with the Lord and His own must be sought in their reluctance to speak about these matters. They complain that they find themselves incapable of expressing their convictions in words. Indeed all of us will find this hard at first. But the oftener a believer gives a reasonable account of the hope that is in him, the easier it will be to witness to the power of God's grace in His life from day to day. In order that the believer may be stimulated, those who conduct family visitation should guard very carefully against doing all the speaking. The visit should never become a one-sided discourse by minister or elder on the Christian life.

[1]John 13:12-17.

(2) Moreover, these visits will build up the confidence of the people in the leadership of the church.

The task of the elders is far from easy and pleasant. Many problems confront them, if they are zealous in keeping the church pure. Thus their decisions are often mercilessly criticized, and misunderstanding of consistorial action has robbed many a congregation of the blessing of living in the unity of the faith. Much of this can be obviated, if there is close contact between consistory and congregation.

Although the elders are always responsible first of all to the Head and King of the church for what they do, we ought not forget that they are elected by the congregation and therefore ought to be able to give a good account of their work to those who are entitled to that knowledge. If the members see the elders in their official capacity only at the time of public worship, the distance between the two parties will likely breed distrust and misunderstanding.

(3) The preventative work in which the elders engage at the time of family visitation will help the believers live more consistently Christian lives.

There are times when God's people stumble into grievous sins before they are fully aware of the net which Satan has spread for them. The longer any particular sin has dominion over their lives, the more hardened their hearts will be, and the more difficult to break with that form of evil. Many will testify that the kindly words and fervent prayers of the elders have greatly aided them in escaping the snares of the devil and restoring them to the blessed fellowship of God.

(4) As a result, this work always presents a good opportunity for learning more about the Christian way of life.

It is at times difficult to see the implications of the gospel for daily life. Although words are wonderful vehicles for the communication of thought, we are still in an imperfect world. Therefore what may be clear to most of the members is by no means plain to all. These latter should be helped. Paul speaks to the elders at Miletus of his practice of going from house to house teaching publicly the things of the kingdom of God. Although the form will be different today, since we have regularly established churches, the church still needs shepherds who teach in the homes of the members.

(5) Finally, by contacting the families in this way, the elders can effectively point out the high ideal of living together as a Christian family from day to day. That our people need such repeated and personal reminders needs no proof.

No congregation is stronger than the families which constitute it. We have the beautiful New Testament picture of churches meeting in the several homes. Even though such an arrangement is quite impractical today and fraught with grave dangers, we may never forget that every Christian family is ideally speaking a miniature church. What greater blessing can be enjoyed than that of seeing God's grace working in the generations, so that grandparents and parents and children alike bow to the same God and Father of our Lord Jesus Christ, rejoice in the same heavenly Savior and experience the gracious operation of the same Holy Spirit? How greatly Paul rejoiced, when he could write to Timothy that once and again he was "reminded of the unfeigned faith that is in thee; which dwelt first in thy grandmother Lois, and thy mother Eunice; and, I am persuaded, in thee also."[1]

We can hardly overestimate the significance of the Christian family for the life of the individual believer. Our first religious impressions were gleaned at the time of family worship. Our childish lips learned first to pray to God at our mothers' knees. There we heard first the stories of the holy gospel and the way of salvation. In general the strongest and sweetest Christian lives are early molded in and by the most spiritual families. Our God is the God of the covenant, whose gracious promises to our children place us under solemn obligation to nurture them in the fear and admonition of the Lord. This is not only sound psychology but above all good Scripture doctrine.

Let the elders never weary of pointing out to children and parents alike their privileges and obligations. The whole Bible plainly teaches the significance of a truly godly home. And when our homes are permeated with the principles of the holy gospel, the future of the church is secure.

If family visitation did no more than keep alive in the minds and hearts of believers the ideal of a truly God-centered home, its value could never be overestimated.

---

[1]II Timothy 1:5.

THE PROPER PRACTICE OF FAMILY VISITATION

"I have now, brethren, done with my advice, and leave you to the practice. Though the proud receive it with scorn, and the selfish and slothful with distaste, or even with indignation, I doubt not but God will use it, in despite of the opposition of sin and Satan, to the awakening of many of his servants to their duty, and to the promotion of a work of right reformation; and that his blessing will accompany the present undertaking for the saving of many souls, the peace of you that understand and perform it, the exciting of his servants throughout the nation to second you, and the increase of the purity and unity of his churches. Amen."

RICHARD BAXTER: THE REFORMED PASTOR.

We have considered at great length some of the basic principles of family visitation. This, however, will not be sufficient to carry the work out successfully. It is necessary to give some time and consideration to the question of its proper exercise also. Unless we are able to give a good account of the work itself, understanding what is required of both elders and members of the congregation, our efforts will be fruitless.

Preparing for the Work

To conduct family visitation successfully the elders ought to prepare themselves carefully for this important task.

It goes without saying, of course, that we who are Reformed are very averse to anything which would smack of legalism in our family visitation. The work is spiritual; therefore so difficult of accomplishment. For that reason we have never countenanced the Roman Catholic practice of supplying prepared manuals, the use of which would be obligatory. For spiritual life we can only lay down general principles. There cannot be specific applications binding equally under any and all circumstances.

God has also been pleased to glorify Himself in the variety of spiritual life found among His people. No two of His children have identical problems and experiences. Therefore the specific approach also at family visitation will have to be left always to the discretion of those elders who engage in the work.

In consequence, preparation for this work will necessarily be of a rather general nature. The elders will not be able to decide beforehand just what they shall say and do. A detailed plan of procedure would be of value only if we could predict with reasonable accuracy how the members of the congregation react under certain circumstances. Since the depths of the heart are known to God alone and only some small part is revealed at any time, we will have to rely upon the Holy Spirit for wisdom and guidance in approaching the needs of the people.

To be conscious of this situation challenges the elders to prepare their own hearts first.

Richard Baxter in his valuable, if somewhat antiquated, work on *The Reformed Pastor* beautifully delineates the spiritual oversight which the pastors (also elders) should have of themselves. According to this worthy divine it consists of five chief parts:

I. See that the work of grace be thoroughly wrought in your own souls.

II. See that you be not only in a state of grace, but that your graces are in vigorous and lively exercise.

III. See that your example contradict not your doctrine.

IV. See that you live not in those sins against which you preach in others.

V. See that you want (lack) not the qualifications necessary for the work.[1]

Only those who are conscious of their own spiritual state of grace can perform this arduous work. They should engage in prayer for guidance before they begin, earnestly beseeching God that the words to be spoken may meet with divine approval and prove to be a blessing to those toward whom they are directed. Any unkind word or gesture may easily prove to be a serious obstacle to the successful conducting of the work.

Let not one of the elders fail to give himself a good account of his personal attitude towards the brethren and sisters. Any censoriousness is out of place. Likewise will those fail who exercise the oversight in the spirit of superiority and tyranny.

But that the chief blessings may be insured, the elders ought not to fail to study the Word of God in which are hidden all the treasures of wisdom and knowledge. Only in its light will we be able to understand the spiritual problems which our people face daily. There will also be abundant occasion for defending the true faith against

[1]Baxter: *The Reformed Pastor*, p. xi.

the false doctrines which are so popular today. In order to teach wisely and well, the elders must be grounded in the faith and have the ability to defend the truth as it is in Christ Jesus with tact and conviction.

Too often family visitation tends to degenerate into a social call. Then it is time and effort wasted to call upon all the members each year. But if we remember the spiritual duty of exercising oversight in the name of Christ, we will not be remiss in preparing ourselves for this work, knowing that no one is sufficient to these things of himself.

Choosing the Best Method

But how must the work be conducted, when the elders arrive at the homes of the members?

This involves the problem of the most advantageous method.

Should the elders ask questions and then expect direct answers, in order to become better acquainted with the spiritual level of the members? Or should they allow the discussion to follow the course decided by those whom they visit?

That there are arguments which can be adduced in favor of the latter practice is self-evident. Particularly when Christians are somewhat advanced in the way of sanctification, it is gratifying to allow them to direct the discussion. They will naturally bring up those matters which they feel to be of greatest concern to themselves and their families. Especially when they are fully conscious of the proper spiritual relationship which should obtain between the members and the officers of the church at the time of family visitation, this method can be successfully pursued. Thus we escape the difficulty of having the work assume the form of inquisition to any degree.

But we should not forget that most people are not able to direct a spiritual discussion profitably. Many times they do not see and understand their own needs as well as the elders do, whose calling it is to watch for their souls. Never may we lose sight of the distinction between official family visitation and free spiritual discussion between the brethren of the church for mutual edification. The former seeks not only the profit of the individual but above all the growth of the whole body of Christ in truth and love.

Bearing these things in mind, we will understand the necessity of carefully considering the questions which should be asked and answered.

Suggestions by Certain Reformed Fathers

Biesterveld in his work on family visitation mentions what some Reformed writers considered to be proper and necessary questions at the time of these visits.

Zepperus, for example, thought that the minister ought to ask about the knowledge which each member had of the Reformed faith, also whether family worship and catechism teaching in the home were maintained, and further whether the members diligently attended the preaching of the Word and partook when the Lord's Supper was administered.

Helmichius strongly stressed the personal character of the work and considered it essential that family visitation be used to bring the wandering sheep back to the fold. He regards the pastor as the physician of souls who must prescribe the spiritual medicines and as jurist who can help the believers in their difficulties.

William Teelinck, Reformed pastor at Middelburg during the first quarter of the seventeenth century, speaks of the profitableness of carrying on family visitation at the time of the celebration of the Lord's Supper. Already in his days some were beginning to depart from this practice, which he considered a grievous loss for the spiritual welfare of the congregation.

One of the most complete discussions of this official work is to be found in the works of Voetius. He speaks of two types of visitation; the regular visitation by the ministers and elders before each celebration of the Lord's Supper, and the occasional visitation (*visitatio occasionata*) which ought to take place at least once each year. Upon the first occasion three matters were to be considered: first, whether the believers understood and practiced the proper preparation for and use of the Holy Supper; then, whether the religious services in the church were attended and godliness was practiced in the home; and finally, whether the believers lived in harmony with their neighbors. If the results were unfavorable, the consistory was obliged to continue its labors regularly with such a family until a change for the better took place. At the time of the occasional visitation the pastor was to ask more confidentially about the spiritual condition of each member of the family. Thus the sorrowing were comforted, the weak in faith encouraged, and the wayward warned.

This list could be considerably lengthened, but surely the above is sufficient to suggest the direction taken by leaders in the Reformed churches in the period of their greatest influence and prosperity.

In times past some have drawn up series of questions which could serve as guides to the elders. Never were these meant to be followed rigidly and in routine fashion. Yet in so far as they were used as guides, they served an admirable purpose. Two of these we would include here, in order that their value may not be lost. It should be remembered that they reflect the social and spiritual conditions of the times in which they were written and therefore can hardly be considered satisfactory in that form for us today. New problems have arisen, and these too should be faced. However, because of their value we would include the two given by Biesterveld.

In the year 1708 the Synod of Glasgow in Scotland passed an act respecting "Ministerial Visitation." By it the visitation of all the families in every parish was regulated for the Scotch churches. The following manner of procedure was prescribed:

1. After the minister has received a list of all the persons in the family, he is to speak to all in a general way about the necessity of regeneration and the examples of sincere, religious and pious living; also about piety towards God and righteousness and mercy towards men.
2. Then more specifically to the servants; about their duty to serve God and to be conscientious, faithful and obedient servants, and about the reward which is given to all such; commending to them the reading of the Scriptures and prayer, and exhorting them to love and unity, and above all to give diligence to hallowing the day of the Lord.
3. The minister is also to address the children according to their ability to understand, speaking to them of the profit of knowing and loving and serving the Lord in the days of their youth and of honoring their parents, reminding them how they were presented to the Lord in baptism; when they are older and have been instructed in the nature of the Covenant of Grace and its seals, to admonish them personally to devote their lives to God, to desire and prepare for their first celebra-

tion of the Lord's Supper, likewise to read the Scriptures daily, to engage in personal prayers and to hallow the day of the Lord.

4. After the minister has spoken to the servants and children, he must address himself especially to the master and mistress of the family about their personal obligations to God and their care for the salvation of their souls; their duty to promote the true religion and worship of God in their home, opposing and punishing sin, promoting true godliness, and honoring the day of the Lord. Here it is also proper to admonish the fathers to see to it that in the daily family worship the Lord is served in prayer, thanksgiving and Scripture reading.

   Furthermore the minister must ask about the conduct of the servants and the fulfillment of their duties towards God and man, likewise how faithfully they attend family worship and public worship on the Lord's Day, and whether some are godly and sincere. Then, too, whether the ignorant and weak are instructed, and whether proper care is exercised for the training of the children; especially whether they are sent to school, what profit they derive therefrom and how they spend the day of the Lord in the home and in private after the sermon. Together with all this the minister must add appropriate encouragements, directions and admonitions, as he sees fit.

5. The minister is also to inquire about the supply of Bibles.
6. He must admonish the communicants to remember and to pay their vows.
7. And because all this requires much care and zeal towards God and love for the souls of men, it must be done in dependence upon God and with fervent prayer to Him, both before the minister goes out to do this work, and when he is with those whom he visits.[1]

The same author has also provided us with a copy of the resolution adopted by the consistory of the Reformed church of Utrecht about fifty years ago. This action was taken to facilitate the work of family visitation by the elders and the ministers by following a rather well-defined pattern. If we bear in mind the size of such a

[1]Biesterveld: *Het Huisbezoek*, p. 251-253.

congregation, we will understand why such a decision was necessary to give more unity to the work.

Questions which the Elders of the church at Utrecht are to ask the members of the congregation at the time of family visitation:

1. How many constitute the particular family and who these individuals are (father, mother, children, servants, others);
2. Whether all the members of the family have received Holy Baptism;
3. Whether all the members of the family have placed themselves under the supervision of the consistory;
4. Which members of the family have been permitted to partake of the Holy Supper;
5. Whether all the members of the family faithfully attend public worship, especially on the Lord's Day, and as far as this is possible also during the week; whether there is growth in the knowledge of the truth; and whether the head of the family investigates this, particularly on the Lord's Day;
6. Whether all children of school age attend the Christian School, and if not, what reasons are given for this;
7. Whether the members of the family who do not yet attend the Lord's Supper faithfully attend catechetical classes; whether the head of the family supervises their preparation for this; and whether he is acquainted with the fruits of that work;
8. Whether those who have been permitted to come to the Lord's Supper also faithfully make use of this means of grace; and whether the father and mother of the family set a good example in this respect;
9. How those who are under church discipline are conducting themselves (this to be done in private, especially in the case of those who are under silent censure);
10. Whether the head of the family faithfully leads the family in prayer and in teaching them the Word;
11. Whether the children and servants manifest obedience to the fifth commandment;
12. Whether there are any children away from home, and if so, in what circumstances they find themselves; whether these

have already made profession of their faith; whether they faithfully attend the services where they are;

13. How the head of the family watches for the spiritual welfare of the servants which may be in the home;
14. Whether there is any difficulty or trouble in the home, and whether the members live in peace and unity with their neighbors and the members of the church;
15. How the family conducts itself on the Lord's Day;
16. Whether the family according to its ability supports the poor and the church;
17. Whether the family in any way needs the advice or help of the consistory.[1]

Following a Definite Plan

Although the Reformed churches have been opposed to the routine use of prepared manuals for the conducting of family visitation, they as a general rule insisted that some definite plan be followed. Time and again the synods took up the matter and issued certain directives for the proper execution of this work. It is therefore not amiss that we also give some consideration to the definite plan which may be followed with profit.

First of all there are certain preliminary considerations. Those who engage in the work must know how many members constitute the family and approximately how old each one is. This knowledge should properly be gleaned from the church records before the visit. So, too, it is of great help to know something of the spiritual background of the particular family. Have they been members of the church for years, or are they recently converted to the Lord? There is a danger that the visits become mere repetitions of previous calls, especially in the larger congregations where it is practically impossible for every elder to become acquainted with the whole church. This obstacle may be overcome to a degree, if the elders are assigned to certain districts each year and if the consistory insists on reports when family visitation is completed. If these facts are borne in mind, the elders will be better prepared to meet the needs of the family.

But how shall they begin? This is perhaps the most difficult part of the whole work. It is so easy to make a few remarks about

[1]Biestenveld: *Het Huisbezoek*, p. 254-255.

work or weather, with the result that most of the time is consumed with matters that only very indirectly concern family visitation.

Some have profitably made use of prayer at the very beginning. This is appropriate indeed, especially since it reminds both elders and members that the work will not attain its goal unless the Lord gives His blessing. Others have suggested beginning with the reading of an appropriate passage of Scripture, which then serves as the point of departure for the whole discussion. There are, however, certain difficulties which this practice presents. If the reading is to serve its purpose, the passage ought to be particularly appropriate for that family — not some general passage which might be discussed by anyone. Family visitation is to be distinguished from the preaching of the Word precisely in its more personal and direct application of the gospel to our lives. But also, there is the danger that the one who reads begins to comment on the passage, with the result that most of the time is consumed by the exhortation and the elders do not get to know the spiritual condition of the family at all.

If the congregation understands the nature and purpose of these calls, it is not awkward to begin with a direct question to one of the members of the family. And in order that the discussion may be guided properly, some of the following questions ought to be asked.

There are first of all questions of a general nature which should be asked of all. (1) Are all the members faithful in attending divine worship and using the means of grace? That this comes first occasions no surprise. From the lips of the members themselves the officers should know whether they are interested in the service of the Lord. (2) Is there a measure of spiritual growth with each according to age and circumstances? To be able to ask this question properly the elder himself should understand the nature of spiritual life in its several manifestations. We may not expect, as a general rule, the same clear testimony from the young Christians as from those of a more mature age. Although Christ should be personally known and loved and served by all, Christian knowledge and experience deepens as the years go by. (3) Is there peace and unity in the home? Do the several members manifest love and helpfulness in their relations to each other? Often disharmony in the home will do great damage to the tender plant of faith. How careful particularly the father and mother should be in setting an example of love and godliness in the home! (4) Are spiritual matters discussed in the home, especially on the Lord's day? Where secularism so strongly prevails today and threatens the church with undoing, it is necessary to insist on the cultivation of this Christian virtue. Also in connection with this, is provision made for good reading material for old and young alike? We are living in an age, when the printed page is very influential. Books and magazines of all sorts find their way into our homes. Does the father supervise the reading of his children, especially of the young people? Nor is it inappropriate to ask whether what is heard over the radio, particularly on the Lord's day, contributes to the spiritual edification of the family. (5) Is family worship faithfully and profitably conducted? This of course requires ideally that the father leads in audible prayer, reads the Scriptures reverently and if possible comments on the significance of the passage for the family. Likewise, the elders should know whether every member of the family, even the younger children who have learned to read, are in possession of a Bible and make diligent use of it for themselves. (6) Do the children and young people who have not yet professed Christ in the church faithfully attend the catechetical classes? Is their study properly supervised by one or both of the parents? Does the father speak especially to the young people of his family about the necessity and privilege of confessing Christ before men, also warning his children of the sin of breaking the covenant of the Lord? (7) Does the proper spiritual relation exist between the members and the church, particularly the officers? Do the parents by their words and works set an example of honoring the minister, the elders and the deacons for the sake of the holy offices to which these men have been called? (8) Do the members of the family make use of the societies? Also this opportunity for spiritual development should receive greater appreciation by our people. The elders ought to stress the value of such Bible study as well as of the Christian fellowship which is enjoyed at such meetings. (9) What is the relation of the family to the neighbors? This includes not only those who are members of Christ's church, but also unbelievers. Do the members of the family witness for Christ whenever and wherever possible? (10) How do the several members of the family conduct themselves in their daily life? Are they aware that they are "living epistles, read of all men?" The elders can do much to instil in the minds and hearts of the believers the consciousness that all of life must be controlled by the Word, and that one's daily work is a vocation of the Lord. (11) Does the family faithfully and according to its ability support the causes of the kingdom of God? These gifts should be preceded and accompanied by personal prayers. Likewise, the parents should be asked whether they teach their children Christian stewardship, so that when these grow up and make their own living, they realize their obligations to God in financial matters too. (12) Does the head of the family try to promote the sense of true Christian distinctiveness among the various members, especially the young people?

There will of course be other questions which should be asked. First of all, the elders should direct their attention to the father and satisfy themselves that he is faithfully seeking to do his duty. (1) Is he mindful of his position as the head of the family, and does he daily strive to do justice to the obligations involved? (2) Is his authority in the home properly respected by all? (3) Does he execute his priestly duties in the home, praying for himself and his family and the church both privately and publicly? (4) Does he concern himself with the spiritual development of his wife and children, also seeing to it that the children faithfully attend church and catechetical classes and providing them with good Christian literature in the home? (5) Does he see to it that the Christian school is attended? If not, why not? (6) Does he set a good example in his personal life and in his relations to his family and his neighbors?

For the mother there are also certain questions. (1) Is she as a Christian mother aware of her position and influence in the family, especially in regard to the training of the children? (2) Does she seek to assist her husband in every way possible in his important work as head of the home? (3) Does she give all her time to her calling as wife and mother? If not, are there legitimate reasons for her to seek employment outside the home? Is she aware of the peculiar difficulties involved in trying to be gainfully employed and still keep up her home? Does her home, particularly the children, suffer in any way, if this is the case?

Also the children are to be addressed. Some of the questions which may be asked of them include the following. (1) Are they obedient to their parents and superiors, for the Lord's sake? (2) Are they conscious of their peculiar covenant relationship to God? Here the parents have a great obligation, since they have promised to train their children in the ways of the Lord and to explain to them the way of salvation. (3) Are they faithful in attending the catechetical classes, and do they benefit from these as well as from the preaching of the Word in accordance with their age and training? (4) Are the young people preparing for profession of faith? (5) Do they understand the church's position on the Christian's relation to the world in general and to the use of amusements in particular? (6) For what calling in life are they preparing themselves? Have they given any consideration to the possibility of entering full-time Kingdom service in one form or another?

It must be recognized that this list is merely suggestive. Simply to follow a set of questions, no matter how excellent and exhaustive, would breed formalism and legalism of the worst sort. But even though the above list is rather incomplete, it will not be possible to ask and answer the questions above within the space of an hour, if each question receives a fair share of attention. For that reason the elders should know what has been considered previously, if this is at all possible.

Once again, those who conduct the visitation must be filled with deep love for the whole flock of Christ over which they have been placed. As the Great Shepherd knows His own and calls them by name, so should the undershepherds be acquainted with all and thus be able to guide and comfort them according to need.

No man is sufficient to these things of himself. Here a thorough understanding of the Scriptures must be combined with practical wisdom which knows the wrestlings of spiritual life, patience which is able to lead the erring sinner back to the fold, firmness necessary to oppose all sin and keep the church pure, love for the brethren and sisters in spite of all the weaknesses and failings which they may display, and boundless zeal for the glory of God. Yet no elder need perform this work in his own strength. If we lack wisdom, let us with confidence ask God who giveth liberally and upbraideth not. He will supply all our needs, even to putting the words into our mouths. But this demands diligent study of the Word of God and fervent prayer when we engage in His work. Those who do these things will be able to say with the apostle, "But our sufficiency is from God."[1]

---

[1] II Corinthians 3:5.

THE SUPREME IDEAL OF FAMILY VISITATION

"As the people of Israel, after being delivered from the oppression of Egypt, were in advance day by day on the way to their goal, the land of Canaan, so we also must make a steady advance on the way to perfection. The longer we are on the way of eternal life, the nearer we are to be to our ideal!
"Is this indeed a DEMAND?
"No. Thank God! it is a PROMISE."

J. J. KNAP: SPIRITUAL GROWTH.

God's people are strangers and pilgrims in the earth.

Called out of darkness to the marvelous light of the kingdom of heaven, they have the supreme obligation and privilege of showing forth the excellencies of their heavenly Father. In thought, word and deed their lives are to be transformed after the pattern and image of the Lord Jesus, through whose precious blood they have their redemption from sin and through the power of whose Holy Spirit they are kept for the salvation ready to be revealed in the last times.

All of their life must therefore come under the sweet and pervasive influence of His Word, which is the rule for their faith and practice. How earnestly they learn to pray,

Fill Thou my life, O Lord, my God,
  In every part with praise;
That my whole being may proclaim
  Thy being and Thy ways.
Not for the lip of praise alone,
  Nor e'en the praising heart,
I ask, but for a life made up
  Of praise in every part.

Praise in the common words I speak,
  Life's common looks and tones,
In intercourse at hearth and board
  With my beloved ones,
Enduring wrong, reproach or loss,
  With sweet and steadfast will,
Loving and blessing those who hate,
  Returning good for ill.

So shall each fear, each fret, each care,
  Be turned into a song,
And every winding of the way
  The echo shall prolong;
So shall no part of day or night
  From sacredness be free,
But all my life in every step,
  Be fellowship with Thee.

This is not only a most complete ideal but also a most difficult program to be realized. For within us we still find in this life the power of sin. Daily is necessity laid upon us to mortify the flesh and walk in newness of life. From without continual temptations force themselves upon us, against which we, except for the grace of God, are absolutely powerless. This constant struggle must teach us each day anew our own unworthiness and helplessness. Faced with such undeniable spiritual realities, we are to seek refuge always in our blessed Savior through Whom we have the power to a new life.

This santification continues as long as we are in this life. Indeed, the way is not one of unbroken progress. Often and even bitterly the children of God complain that the good that they would, they do not, and the evil that they would not, they do. There are seasons of spiritual barrenness, lean years in our lives, when we see so little of the power of sovereign grace and taste so seldom the preciousness of the divine presence. There are days of murmuring and rebellion against the mysterious ways of the overruling providence. There are moments of despair, when we feel ourselves dreadfully lost in the mazes of sin. And yet in and through all this our faithful Covenant God continues to work out the salvation of His own. Never does He forsake the works of His own hands. Step by step He leads us along the way with all its trials and temptations, until after life's little day is past we are meet for full fellowship with Him in glory.

Thus the Christian life below is a preparation for eternity. God has been pleased to work the first principles of grace in His own at the time of their regeneration. And as this life which He begets begins to unfold itself and becomes conscious of these tremendous spiritual realities, it needs direction and encouragement. Such is the pastoral duty of the overseers of the flock of Christ. Being themselves rooted and grounded in His Word and enjoying the assurance that they belong to the Savior, they are used to build up the church on earth.

They must instruct the congregation. In season and out of season their calling requires them to hold before every member the word of life which alone can make sinners wise unto salvation.

They must rebuke those who err. Young and old alike stray from the paths of righteousness and seek their fulfillment at times in the fields of sin. Lovingly, but firmly, the undershepherds seek such erring sheep and lead them back to the shelter of the fold, where alone there is safety and security.

They must comfort. Life may seem to deal bitterly with God's children for a season. The chastisements which come to each in His own time are grievous to be borne. Yet God wills that none shall be tempted above that which can be endured and therefore He commissions His servants to speak words of consolation and cheer. Being so strengthened and encouraged His people are able to continue their journey joyfully.

Does such spiritual work bear fruit? Indeed, it must. This cannot be otherwise, since God's Word never returns to Him void but accomplishes that whereunto it was sent. The saints are built up in faith and are drawn into ever closer communion with Him who is the fountain-head and final goal of their lives. Sinners who harden themselves against godly counsel and reproof are exposed and, unless they return to the Lord, must be excommunicated from the church, so that the body of Christ may be kept pure. Going from strength to strength in loving and obedient service to God through Christ, the congregation already here receives a foretaste of heaven.

And when eternity breaks, the results of this spiritual work of the officers of the church will be made manifest in the redeemed multitude which praises its God and Savior in perfection. The word of God by the mouth of His servant Daniel must be fulfilled: "And many of them that sleep in the dust of the earth shall awake, some to everlasting life, and some to shame and everlasting contempt. And they that are wise shall shine as the brightness of the firmament, and they that turn many to righteousness as the stars forever and ever."[1]

[1]Daniel 12:2, 3.

www.ingramcontent.com/pod-product-compliance
Lightning Source LLC
LaVergne TN
LVHW020654100826
845148LV00012B/2491

* 9 7 8 1 5 9 2 4 4 4 4 9 6 *